Breakfast & Brunch Dishes

for the Professional Chef

Terence Janericco

CBI

A CBI Book
Published by Van Nostrand Reinhold Company

A CBI Book
(CBI is an imprint of Van Nostrand Reinhold Company Inc.)

Copyright © 1983 by Van Nostrand Reinhold Company

Library of Congress Catalog Card Number

ISBN 0-8436-2256-3

Van Nostrand Reinhold Company Inc.
135 West 50th Street
New York, New York 10020

Van Nostrand Reinhold Company Limited
Molly Millars Lane
Wokingham, Berkshire RG11 2PY, England

Van Nostrand Reinhold
480 La Trobe Street
Melbourne, Victoria 3000, Australia

Macmillan of Canada
Division of Gage Publishing Limited
164 Commander Boulevard
Agincourt, Ontario M1S 3C7, Canada

16 15 14 13 12 11 10 9 8 7 6 5 4 3 2

Library of Congress Cataloging in Publication Data

Janericco, Terence.
    Breakfast & brunch dishes for the professional chef.

    Includes index.
    1. Breakfasts.   2. Brunches.   3. Quantity
cookery. I. Title. II. Title Breakfast and
brunch dishes for the professional chef.
TX733.J36 1983   641.57   82-4542
ISBN 0-8436-2256-3   AACR2

Contents

084198

To the many people who have encouraged and supported me in my career as an apprentice, cook, researcher, teacher, and writer, I give my deepest thanks.

In particular, this book is dedicated to those persons who have given me the free use of their restaurants to prepare and serve these dishes on so many occasions.

Alice Foreman MacSorley
Vincent Salmonte
Thomas McMullen

Introduction

Breakfasts and brunches have become increasingly important in the creation of profits for all restaurants and hotels. Dining rooms that were left vacant during these hours are filling up with customers, who come not only for a bare egg, a strip of bacon, and a piece of toast, but often for the much more elaborate offerings of a brunch. The customers are ready and willing to pay a premium for a more interesting brunch menu.

What makes this most pleasing for professional chefs is that it allows them to offset some of the problems of food costs for other meals. For the most part, the food used in brunches is low cost and only a minimum staff is required. Very often it is possible to use the leftovers from previous meals, especially those from major banquets and receptions. The intelligent, creative chef will quickly learn that a great deal of money, which was discarded in the form of leftovers, can now be turned into profits.

Because you can use low-budget foods, it is possible to appear lavish in your offerings, at minimal cost. One of the most important points is that this food very often is the first meal of the day for the customer and therefore should look inviting, interesting, and appealing. If your staff serves unappealing dishes, in the first light of the day this meal will appear even more unpleasant than it is. Always try to make food look attractive, especially these important first meals.

This book gives you recipes for numerous brunch and breakfast dishes along with photographs to guide you and your staff in presenting the food attractively.

Eggs Benedict

1 English muffin, split, toasted

2 thin slices Canadian bacon, heated

2 poached eggs, drained

2 ounces Hollandaise sauce

black olive or truffle cutouts, optional

Arrange muffins on a serving plate. Top with bacon and eggs. Coat with sauce. Garnish with olive or truffle cutouts.

Note: An American dish, this is never listed as Oeufs a la Benedictine.

Oeufs Poches a la Florentine

Eggs Florentine

4 ounces creamed spinach

2 poached eggs

2 ounces Mornay sauce

1 tablespoon grated Gruyere or Parmesan

1 tablespoon buttered bread crumbs

Place spinach in bottom of casserole. Top with eggs, coat with sauce, and sprinkle top with cheese and bread crumbs. Glaze.

Chapter 1

Poached Eggs
hot & cold

One of the best-sellers on any brunch menu is Eggs Benedict. Many other poached egg dishes also will have as much appeal once your guests have become familiar with them. For the summer months, cold poached egg dishes can be prepared ahead for ease in serving. They are a refreshing change and can be a stunning addition to the brunch buffet.

Oeufs Poches
Joinville

Poached Eggs Joinville

1/2 cup sauteed croutons
2 poached eggs
2 ounces shrimp veloute
2 shrimp, cooked, shelled
    paprika

Place croutons in a casserole, top with eggs, and coat with sauce. Place a shrimp on top of each egg. Dust with paprika.

Eggs Massena

2 cooked artichoke bottoms
2 tablespoons Bearnaise sauce
2 poached eggs
2 ounces tomato sauce
2 slices poached marrow
    minced parsley

Place artichokes on a plate and coat with Bearnaise. Top with eggs and coat with tomato sauce. Place a slice of marrow on each egg and sprinkle with parsley.

Oeufs Poches
a la Portugaise

Poached Eggs Portuguese Style

3/4 cup cooked rice
1-1/2 tablespoons tomato puree
2 poached eggs
    salt and pepper to taste
1/4 cup Mornay sauce
1/4 cup grated Gruyere

Combine rice and tomato puree. Place in bottom of casserole. Top with eggs and season with salt and pepper. Coat with sauce and dust with cheese. Glaze.

Oeufs Poches a la Milanaise

Poached Eggs Milan Style

- 1/3 pound spaghetti
- salt and pepper to taste
- 2 tablespoons tomato sauce
- 2 tablespoons grated Parmesan
- 2-1/2 tablespoons butter
- 6 poached eggs
- 12 broiled tomato halves

Combine the spaghetti, salt, pepper, tomato sauce, cheese, and butter. Pack into six buttered timbale molds. Bake in bain marie at 350°F. for 18 minutes. Unmold onto a plate. Top with poached eggs and garnish with tomatoes.

Oeufs Poches a l'Andalouse

Poached Eggs Andalouse Style

- 2 sweet green peppers, blanched
- 1 cup rice pilaf
- 2 chicken livers, sauteed, sliced
- 2 poached eggs
- 2 ounces tomato sauce

Fill the peppers with rice mixed with chicken livers. Top with poached eggs and coat with sauce.

1 Poached
Eggs

Oeufs Poches Aurore
Poached Eggs Aurora

2 slices buttered toast
2 poached eggs
  salt and pepper to taste
4 ounces Bechamel sauce
2 tablespoons tomato puree
2 hard cooked egg yolks, sieved

Place the toast on a plate. Top with eggs and season with salt and pepper. Combine Bechamel and tomato puree and coat each egg. Sprinkle with egg yolks.

Oeufs Poches a la Victoria
Poached Eggs Victoria

1/3 cup minced cooked chicken
1/3 cup veloute sauce
2 croustades
12 poached eggs
2 mushroom caps, julienne

Bind the chicken with half of the sauce and fill croustades. Place poached eggs on top and coat with remaining sauce. Garnish with mushroom julienne.

Tschimbur
Poached Eggs with Garlic Yogurt Sauce

2 poached eggs
1/2 cup yogurt
1/2 clove garlic, crushed
  salt and pepper to taste
1-1/2 tablespoons butter
1/2 teaspoon paprika

Place eggs on a dish. Warm yogurt and garlic and season with salt and pepper. Coat eggs. Heat butter and paprika until fragrant. Pour over the eggs.

Oeufs Poches a la Haut Brion

Poached Eggs Haut Brion

2 leeks, julienne

2 tablespoons butter

1/2 cup red Bordeaux

salt, pepper, and nutmeg to taste

1 bouquet garni

1 tablespoon beurre manie

2 sauteed potato cakes

2 ham rounds

6 poached eggs

Sweat leeks in butter until tender. Add wine. Correct seasoning with salt, pepper, and nutmeg. Add bouquet garni. Simmer 30 minutes. Discard bouquet garni. Thicken with beurre manie. Place potato cakes on a plate. Top with ham and eggs. Spoon sauce over all.

Oeufs Poches aux Saumon Fume

Poached Eggs with Smoked Salmon

1 English muffin, split, toasted, buttered

2 slices smoked salmon

2 poached eggs

2 ounces Hollandaise sauce

Place muffins on a plate. Top with salmon and eggs and coat with sauce.

Oeufs Poches au Cari Mayonnaise

Cold Poached Eggs with Curry Mayonnaise

6 cold poached eggs, trimmed

1 cup mayonnaise

curry powder to taste

Arrange eggs in a serving dish. Combine mayonnaise and curry powder and coat eggs. Serve with chutney, salted cashews, toasted coconut, and sieved, hard cooked eggs.

Oeufs Poches Louisiane

Cold Poached Eggs Louisiana

4 hard cooked egg yolks, mashed
1/2 cup chopped pimiento
1/2 cup mayonnaise
1 cup chicken aspic
2 large green peppers, hollowed
8 poached eggs, chilled

Combine yolks, pimientos, mayonnaise, and 2 tablespoons liquid aspic. Stuff peppers and chill until firm. Trim eggs. Cut peppers into 1/2-inch thick slices. Place an egg on each slice. Coat with remaining aspic.

Oeufs Poches Virginia Club

Poached Eggs Virginia Club

2 cups cooked corn kernels
2/3 cup mayonnaise
salt and pepper to taste
6 cold poached eggs, trimmed
watercress
3 medium tomatoes, quartered
olive oil
black olives

Combine corn with 1/4 cup mayonnaise, salt, and pepper. Shape into a base on a dish and chill. Coat eggs with remaining mayonnaise and arrange on corn. Garnish with watercress and tomatoes, seasoned with salt, pepper, and olive oil. Arrange olives.

Oeufs Poches Tartare

Poached Eggs Tartar

- 3 medium tomatoes
- salt and pepper to taste
- 2 cups cold, cooked mixed vegetables
- 2/3 cup mayonnaise
- 6 cold poached eggs, trimmed
- 2 tablespoons minced parsley
- 2 tablespoons minced gherkins
- lettuce

Cut tomatoes in half, scoop out center, and season shells. Dice centers, reserve pulp, and drain. Combine centers with vegetables and 1/4 cup mayonnaise. Fill tomatoes and top with eggs. Coat eggs with remaining mayonnaise. Garnish with parsley and gherkins. Serve on lettuce.

Oeufs aux Crevettes

Cold Eggs with Shrimp

- 6 cold poached eggs, trimmed
- 1/2 pound small shrimp, shelled
- 3/4 cup heavy cream, whipped
- 3/4 cup mayonnaise
- salt and pepper to taste
- 3 tablespoons minced chives or dill

Place eggs in serving dish. Surround with shrimp. Fold cream and mayonnaise together and correct seasoning. Coat eggs. Sprinkle with chives or dill.

1 Poached Eggs

Oeufs Farcis a la Hollandaise

Stuffed Eggs Hollandaise

  12 hard cooked eggs, halved
  1/2 pound mushrooms, minced
  2 tablespoons butter
  4 tablespoons grated Parmesan
  1 tablespoon tomato paste
  1/4 cup heavy cream
  1-1/2 cups Hollandaise sauce

Sieve the yolks. Combine with mushrooms and saute in butter until the liquid has evaporated. Stir in cheese, tomato paste, and cream. Stuff whites. Place eggs in a baking dish and reheat. Top with sauce.

Chapter 2

Hard Cooked Eggs hot & cold

Hard cooked eggs can be an interesting change from poached eggs. They are greatly appreciated by the customer who cannot abide a runny egg. Although hard cooked eggs are often used for cold buffets, there are many hot versions that fit into the year-round brunch menu.

Oeufs Durs Aurore

Hard Cooked Eggs Aurora

6 hard cooked eggs, halved
4 tablespoons butter
1/3 cup tomato sauce
3/4 cup Bechamel sauce
   salt and pepper to taste

Remove yolks from whites and sieve. Add 2 tablespoons of butter, 1 tablespoon tomato sauce, and 1/4 cup Bechamel and correct seasoning. Stuff whites and place in baking dish. Melt remaining butter and pour over eggs. Reheat at 350° F. Combine remaining tomato and Bechamel sauces and heat. Pour over eggs.

Oeufs Dur aux Sauce Moutarde

Hard Cooked Eggs with Mustard Sauce

1 cup Bechamel sauce
1 teaspoon dry mustard
   salt and pepper to taste
6 hard cooked eggs, halved

Heat Bechamel. Stir in mustard, salt, and pepper. Arrange eggs in a shallow dish and pour sauce over them. Glaze.

Oeufs sur le Plat a la
Portugaise
*Shirred Eggs Portuguese
Style*
(See page 24.)

Shrimp with Sour
Cream
(See page 82.)

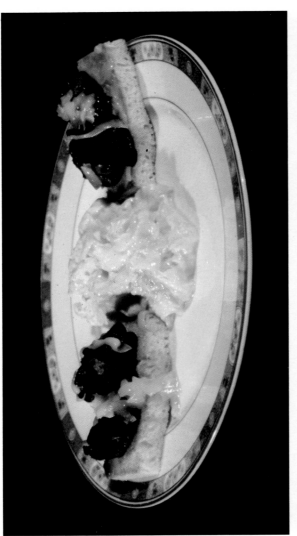

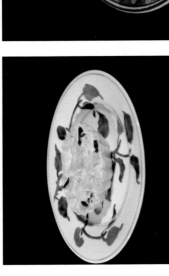

Asparagus Pie
(See page 48.)

Scrambled Eggs with
Snail Toasts
(See page 43.)

Scrambled Eggs in
Tomato Cup
(See page 40.)

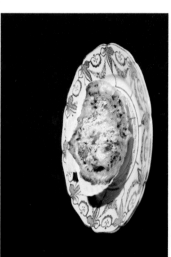

Eggs Borrachos
Shirred Eggs Borrachos
(See page 22.)

Coquilles St. Jacques
au Gratin
Scallops with Mushroom
Duxelles
(See page 78.)

Ham Hash
(See page 97.)

Chicken Livers and
Grapes
(See page 88.)

Eggs with Skordalia
*Eggs with Garlic
Mayonnaise
(See page 16.)*

Lox and Eggs
(See page 42.)

Oeufs sur le Plat a la
Mexicaine
*Shirred Eggs Mexican
Style*
(See page 21.)

Artichoke and
Sausage Quiche
(See page 53.)

Crepazes
(See page 68.)

Oeufs sur le Plat a la
Grecque
Shirred Eggs Greek Style
(See page 24.)

Oeufs Dur Mistral
Hard Cooked Eggs Mistral
(See page 14.)

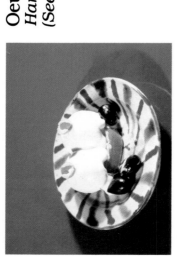

Souffles aux Crevettes
a l'Estragon
Shrimp Souffle with
Tarragon
(See page 59.)

Oeufs Dur a la Bretonne

Hard Cooked Eggs
Brittany Style

2 cups Bechamel sauce

1/2 cup minced onions, sauteed in butter

1/2 cup minced leeks, sauteed in butter

1/2 cup minced mushrooms, sauteed in butter

6 hard cooked eggs, halved

Combine the Bechamel, onions, leeks, and mushrooms. Spoon a layer in the bottom of a baking dish. Top with eggs and coat with remaining sauce. Glaze.

Oeufs Dur aux Olives

Hard Cooked Eggs
with Olives

2 cups Demi-glace sauce

2 egg yolks

1/2 cup black olives, sliced

1 tomato, peeled, seeded, diced

2 tablespoons capers

2 tablespoons lemon juice

salt to taste

12 hard cooked eggs, halved, warmed

Enrich Demi-glace with egg yolks. Stir in olives, tomato, capers, lemon juice, and salt. Heat until hot, but do not boil. Arrange egg halves on a dish and pour sauce over.

Hard 2 Cooked Eggs

Oeufs Durs a la Hongroise

Hungarian Hard Cooked Eggs

6 hard cooked eggs, halved
4 tablespoons minced onion
4 tablespoons butter
1 teaspoon paprika
   salt and pepper to taste
3 ripe tomatoes, 1/2-inch thick
   slices
lemon juice to taste
1/2 cup heavy cream

Remove yolks and sieve. Saute onion in butter until soft. Blend half into yolks with 1/2 teaspoon paprika. Correct seasoning. Fill whites. Saute tomato slices in remaining butter and onion mixture until hot and tender. Place tomatoes in baking dish. Arrange eggs on top. Combine remaining paprika, lemon juice, and cream. Pour over eggs and heat.

Eggs and Oysters

1 tablespoon minced onion
2 tablespoons butter
2 tablespoons vegetable oil
4 tablespoons flour
1 cup water
1 cup oyster liquor
   salt and pepper to taste
24 cooked oysters
6 hard cooked eggs, halved
   boiled rice

Saute onion in butter and oil until golden. Stir in flour and cook roux. Add water and oyster liquor to make a sauce. Simmer 10 minutes. Correct seasoning. Add oysters and eggs. Heat and serve over rice.

Cheese Tomato Eggs

1 onion, minced
3 tablespoons butter
5 cups stewed, drained tomatoes
1 teaspoon chervil
1/2 teaspoon minced basil
1/4 teaspoon salt
4 ounces cream cheese
12 hard cooked eggs, sliced

Saute onion in butter until golden. Stir in tomatoes, chervil, basil, and salt. Reduce to 2 cups. Stir cream cheese into 1/2 cup of sauce until melted. Arrange eggs in serving dishes. Coat with tomato-cheese sauce. Surround with plain tomato sauce. Reheat if necessary.

Oeufs Dur aux Crevettes

Hard Cooked Eggs with Shrimp

6 hard cooked eggs, halved
1 pound shrimp, cooked, peeled, deveined
3/4 cup heavy cream, whipped
3/4 cup mayonnaise
salt and pepper to taste
minced chives or dill

Place eggs, rounded side up, in a serving dish. Garnish with shrimp. Fold cream into mayonnaise and correct seasoning. Coat eggs and sprinkle with chives or dill.

Eggs Huntington

1 cup chicken veloute
4 hard cooked eggs, minced
2 tablespoons grated Parmesan
2 tablespoons pumpernickel bread crumbs

Combine the veloute and eggs and fill ramekins. Sprinkle with cheese and bread crumbs. Glaze.

Meulemeester Eggs

6 hard cooked eggs, chopped
2 ounces butter, melted
1 teaspoon minced parsley
1/2 teaspoon Dijon mustard
1/2 teaspoon minced chervil
12 shrimp, peeled
1 cup heavy cream
   salt and pepper to taste
3 tablespoons grated Gruyere

Combine eggs with 1 ounce of butter, parsley, mustard, chervil, shrimp, cream, salt, and pepper. Arrange in buttered dishes and sprinkle with cheese and remaining butter. Glaze.

Oeufs Dur Mistral

Hard Cooked Eggs Mistral

6 hard cooked eggs, halved
   salt and pepper to taste
1 cup mayonnaise
6 1/2-inch thick tomato slices
3 pimiento-stuffed olives, halved
1/2 cup black olives
   parsley

Sprinkle cut sides of eggs with salt and pepper. Coat rounded sides with mayonnaise and place eggs, cut side down, on tomato slices. Garnish with olive slices, black olives, and parsley.

Oeufs a la Mozart

Hard Cooked Eggs, Mozart

8 hard cooked eggs
  anchovy paste to taste
2-1/2 cups mayonnaise
6 gherkins or spiced cherries
3 tablespoons minced chives
3 tomatoes, peeled, halved, and
  hollowed

Cut 2 eggs in half. Sieve whites. Cut out one quarter of the remaining eggs lengthwise, exposing the yolks. Carefully remove yolks. Mash all yolks with anchovy paste and enough mayonnaise to bind. Pipe mixture into eggs. Decorate yolk with gherkins or cherries and sprinkle with chives. Set cut side up in tomato halves. Sprinkle whites over remaining mayonnaise and pass separately.

Oeufs Farcis a la Printaniere

Stuffed Eggs with
Vegetables and Rice Salad

1 cup cooked cold rice
1/2 cup cooked diced carrots
1/2 cup cooked diced green beans
1/2 cup diced seeded cucumber
1/2 cup diced seeded tomato pulp
1/2 cup tarragon-flavored
  vinaigrette
4 hard cooked eggs, halved
8 tablespoons butter
4 ounces liver pate
4 ounces cream cheese
2 teaspoons tomato paste
  bunch of watercress

Combine the rice, carrots, beans, cucumber, tomato pulp, and vinaigrette. Remove yolks from whites and mash with the butter. Divide in half. Beat liver pate into one half and cream cheese and tomato paste into the other half. Fill half the whites with one of the mixtures and the other half with the other mixture. Arrange rice salad in a dish and surround with eggs. Garnish with watercress.

15

Hard
2 Cooked
Eggs

Eggs with Skordalia

Eggs with Garlic Mayonnaise

6 hard cooked eggs, halved
3 tomatoes, quartered
1/2 cup sun-cured black olives
18 small radishes
4 large cloves garlic
1 egg yolk
    salt and pepper to taste
1/2 cup olive oil
1/4 cup fresh white bread crumbs
1/4 cup ground almonds
    lemon juice to taste
    minced parsley

Arrange eggs, tomatoes, olives, and radishes on serving plates. In a processor puree the garlic. Add egg yolk, salt, and pepper. Add oil as for mayonnaise until thickened. Stir in bread crumbs, almonds, lemon juice, and parsley. Drizzle some sauce over eggs and serve remainder separately.

Oeufs Dur en Tapenade

Hard Cooked Eggs with Olive-Anchovy Sauce

24 black olives, pitted
8 anchovy fillets
3 tablespoons capers, drained
2 ounces tuna fish
1/2 cup olive oil
    lemon juice to taste
    cognac to taste
6 hard cooked eggs, halved
12 1/4-inch thick tomato slices

In a processor, combine olives, anchovies, capers, tuna, and oil to form a thick mixture. Season with lemon juice and cognac. Arrange egg halves on tomato slices and coat with sauce.

Oeufs a la Parisienne

Hard Cooked Eggs Parisian

6 hard cooked eggs, halved
6 tablespoons butter
1 tablespoon minced chives
  salt and pepper to taste
6 peeled tomatoes, halved
  sugar to taste
1/2 teaspoon minced garlic
1-1/2 cups mayonnaise collee
2 tablespoons anchovy paste
1 teaspoon tomato paste
1/2 cup light cream
4 radishes, thinly sliced
2 teaspoons minced parsley
  lemon slices

Mash egg yolks and beat in butter, chives, salt, and pepper. Fill whites. Sprinkle cut side of tomatoes with salt, pepper, sugar, and garlic. Place an egg on top, cut side down. Combine mayonnaise, anchovy paste, tomato paste, and enough light cream to make a fluid sauce. Coat the eggs and tomatoes. Chill until set. Arrange on a platter. Garnish with radish slices, parsley, and lemon slices.

Oeufs Farcis au Cognac

Hard Cooked Eggs with Cognac-Olive Sauce

6 hard cooked eggs, halved
6 black olives, minced
2-1/2 tablespoons capers, minced
4 teaspoons tuna fish
1/2 teaspoon Dijon mustard
  pinch of allspice
2 tablespoons cognac
  black pepper to taste
  olive oil to taste
36 whole capers
3 peeled tomatoes, halved
2 cups cold, cooked green beans
3/4 cup vinaigrette

Mash yolks with olives, minced capers, tuna, mustard, allspice, cognac, plenty of pepper, and just enough oil to bind. Fill eggs, mound into domes. Garnish with three capers on each. Arrange tomato halves on a platter. Toss green beans with enough vinaigrette to coat lightly and put in center of platter. Lightly coat tomatoes with some of the vinaigrette, top with eggs, and coat with remaining vinaigrette.

17

Hard 2 Cooked Eggs

Chapter 3

Shirred & Baked Eggs

S hirred eggs (oeufs sur le plat) used to be very popular but have gone out of favor. However, they are delicious and can help a chef build a reputation for different and excellent brunch offerings. They are particularly suitable for the convention breakfast, when hot food has to be served quickly to large numbers of people.

Oeufs sur le Plat Lyonnaise

Shirred Eggs Lyonnaise Style

2 cups minced onions

4 tablespoons butter

12 eggs

3 cups Lyonnaise sauce

Saute onions in butter until golden. Place in bottom of shirred egg dishes and top with two eggs. Surround with sauce and bake until set.

Oeufs sur le Plat Omar Pascha

Shirred Eggs Omar Pasha

12 tablespoons minced onions

3 tablespoons butter

12 eggs

12 tablespoons grated Parmesan

Sweat onions in butter. Put two tablespoons in each of 6 dishes. Top with eggs and sprinkle with cheese. Bake.

Oeufs sur le Plat aux Champignons, Dit a la Polonaise

Baked Eggs with Mushrooms

1/4 pound mushrooms, sliced, sauteed in butter
1/2 cup Bechamel sauce
1/3 cup light cream
1/2 teaspoon lemon juice
4 large eggs

Combine mushrooms, Bechamel, and cream. Simmer ten minutes. Stir in lemon juice. Pour into 4 dishes, make indentations, and break an egg into each. Season with salt and pepper. Bake until set.

Oeufs sur le Plat a la Catalane

Shirred Eggs Catalonian Style

1 medium eggplant, sliced
3 large tomatoes, sliced
12 tablespoons butter
12 eggs
1 garlic clove, crushed
salt and pepper to taste
minced parsley

Saute eggplant and tomato slices in butter until tender. Remove to shirred egg dishes. Top with eggs. Saute garlic until soft. Season garlic butter with salt and pepper. Sprinkle eggs with garlic butter. Bake until set. Sprinkle with parsley.

Oeufs sur le Plat aux Witloof

Baked Eggs with Braised Endive

12 eggs
6 tablespoons butter
  salt and pepper to taste
6 heads braised endive
1 cup Allemande sauce

Shirr eggs in butter until set. Season with salt and pepper. Divide endive lengthwise and place around eggs. Coat with sauce.

Oeufs sur le Plat a la Mexicaine

Shirred Eggs Mexican Style

12 thin slices bacon, diced
12 tomato slices
6 canned chilies, minced
12 eggs

Crisp the bacon in egg dishes in the oven. Place two tomato slices in each dish and top with 1 tablespoon of minced chili. Add eggs and bake until set.

Baked Eggs Deerfoot

12 breakfast sausages, half cooked
2 teaspoons butter
2 cups tomato sauce
2 teaspoons minced parsley
12 eggs

Combine sausages, butter, and tomato sauce and simmer 10 minutes. Add parsley. Divide among shirred egg dishes. Top with eggs and bake until set.

Shirred & Baked Eggs
3

Oeufs sur le Plat aux Haricot de Lima

Shirred Eggs with Lima Beans

10 ounces cooked lima beans
 salt and pepper to taste
2 tablespoons butter
1 onion, thinly sliced
1 teaspoon minced parsley
1 tomato, peeled and cut in 1/2-inch thick slices

8 eggs
3 tablespoons cream
2 tablespoons grated Parmesan

Season beans with salt and pepper. Sweat onion in butter. Add beans, parsley, and tomato and correct seasoning. Heat. Divide among 4 dishes and top with eggs. Spoon cream over yolks, sprinkle with cheese, and bake.

Oeufs sur le Plat au Fromage

Shirred Eggs with Cheese

6 toast rounds
1/4 cup melted butter
6 slices Gruyere
6 eggs
 salt and pepper to taste
6 tablespoons grated Gruyere

Dip toast rounds in butter and arrange in dishes. Top with a slice of cheese and bake until cheese melts. Put an egg on top of cheese and season with salt and pepper. Sprinkle with grated cheese. Bake until set.

Eggs Borrachos
Shirred Eggs Borrachos

1-1/2 cups lima bean puree
12 slices bacon, cooked
12 eggs
6 tablespoons butter
4 tablespoons dry red wine

Spread puree in bottom of egg dishes. Top with 2 slices of bacon and 2 eggs. Melt butter, beat in wine, and pour over eggs. Bake until set.

Oeufs sur le Plat Flamenco

Shirred Eggs Flamenco

2 cooked potatoes, 1/2-inch cubes

3 sausages, 1/4-inch slices

4 tablespoons butter

2 tablespoons cooked peas

2 canned pimientos, diced
salt and pepper to taste

2 tomatoes, peeled, seeded, diced
1/2 inch

3 tablespoons minced parsley

8 eggs

2 tablespoons heavy cream
cayenne pepper to taste

Brown the potatoes and sausage in butter. Add peas, pimientos, salt, and pepper. Add tomatoes and parsley and mix together. Divide among 4 shirred egg dishes. Place eggs on top and season with salt and pepper. Bake 7 to 8 minutes. Spoon on cream and bake until done. Sprinkle with cayenne.

Oeufs sur le Plat Lully

Shirred Eggs Lully

2 tablespoons butter

12 eggs

12 toast rounds

12 ham rounds, sauteed in butter

2 cups tomatoes, peeled, seeded,
chopped

3 tablespoons butter

1/4 pound very fine egg noodles
(capellini), cooked

Heat 1 teaspoon of butter in each of 6 dishes until hot. Add eggs and bake. Place 2 slices of toast on a serving dish. Top with ham and eggs. Stew tomatoes in butter and toss with capellini. Arrange around eggs.

Shirred
& Baked
3 Eggs

Oeufs sur le Plat a la Portugaise

Shirred Eggs Portuguese Style

6 tablespoons tomato fondue

12 eggs

   salt and pepper to taste

3 cups tomato fondue

   minced parsley

Heat the egg dishes. Place 1 table-spoon of hot tomato fondue in each dish. Add eggs and season with salt and pepper. Bake. Surround eggs with tomato fondue and sprinkle with parsley.

Oeufs sur le Plat a la Grecque

Shirred Eggs Greek Style

4 mushrooms, sliced

6 tablespoons butter

1/2 teaspoon lemon juice

1 small eggplant, diced

2 tablespoons olive oil

   rind of 1 orange, julienne

1/2 teaspoon crushed garlic

1 baking potato, boiled 3 minutes, diced

2 onions, diced

1 green pepper, diced

1 red pepper, diced

2 tomatoes, peeled, chopped

   salt and pepper to taste

12 eggs

Saute mushrooms in 3 tablespoons of butter and lemon juice. Set aside. Brown eggplant in olive oil. Saute orange rind and garlic in remaining butter over low heat 2 minutes. Add potato and cook 3 minutes. Add onions and simmer 2 minutes. Add peppers and saute 2 minutes. Add eggplant, mushrooms, and tomatoes and correct seasoning. Divide among shirred egg dishes. Top with eggs and bake.

Oeufs Brayen

Baked Eggs Brayen

6 eggs
6 tablespoons heavy cream
  salt and pepper to taste
6 slices buttered toast
1 cup Bechamel sauce
  minced parsley

Beat eggs, cream, salt, and pepper. Pour into buttered ramekins. Bake in water bath until set. Turn out onto toast slices. Coat with Bechamel and sprinkle with parsley.

Oeufs en Cocotte

Baked Eggs

1 cup celery puree
1/2 cup cream sauce
6 eggs
  salt and pepper to taste
3 tablespoons heavy cream
  minced chervil

Combine celery puree and cream sauce and divide among 6 custard cups. Break an egg into each cup and season with salt and pepper. Place cups in a water bath. Bake until set. Before serving coat with cream and sprinkle with chervil.

Shirred & Baked Eggs 3

Gebakken Eiren mit Wien en Kaas

Baked Eggs with Wine in Cheese

1/2 cup cream
4 tablespoons grated Gruyere
2 tablespoons lemon juice
2 tablespoons dry white wine
  Dijon mustard to taste
  salt and pepper to taste
8 eggs
  buttered bread crumbs

Combine cream, cheese, lemon juice, and wine. Stir in mustard, salt, and pepper. Break 2 eggs into each ramekin, cover with sauce, and sprinkle with buttered bread crumbs. Place in water bath and bake until set.

Spanish Eggs

2 cups beef stock, unsalted
1/4 cup butter
1 cup minced lean pork
2 cups minced ham
1/2 cup minced onion
1/4 cup flour
3 large tomatoes, peeled, seeded, chopped
  salt and pepper to taste
6 eggs
  minced parsley

Reduce beef stock to 1 cup. Saute pork, ham, and onion in butter until lightly browned. Add enough beef stock to the flour to make a slurry and stir into the ham mixture. Add remaining stock and tomatoes, blending well. Correct seasoning. Simmer until thickened. Place in ramekins. Top with eggs and bake in water bath until set. Garnish with parsley.

Oeufs en Cocotte Lorraine

Baked Eggs Lorraine

6 teaspoons diced, fried bacon
18 thin slices Gruyere
6 tablespoons boiling cream
12 eggs
   salt and pepper to taste

Place a teaspoon of bacon in each ramekin. Cover with 3 slices Gruyere and top with 1 tablespoon cream. Break in two eggs and season with salt and pepper. Bake in water bath until set.

Oeufs en Surprise

Eggs in Tomato Cases

4 medium tomatoes
   salt and pepper to taste
   butter
4 teaspoons minced onion
4 teaspoons minced parsley
4 eggs
1/4 cup bread crumbs
2 tablespoons grated Parmesan
4 teaspoons oil

Remove tops from tomatoes and scoop out centers. Drain, season with salt and pepper, and place in buttered casserole. Put a teaspoon of onion and parsley in each tomato. Break an egg into each and cover with crumbs and cheese. Drizzle with oil. Bake until egg is set.

Corned Beef Hash with Eggs

1-1/2 cups finely chopped corned beef

2 cups finely chopped boiled potatoes

1 tablespoon chopped onions

1/3 cup cream

salt and pepper to taste

2 tablespoons butter

6 eggs

Combine beef, potatoes, onions, cream, salt, and pepper. Shape into 3-inch round patties, 1 inch thick. Arrange in buttered baking dishes. Make a hollow in each. Break egg into hollow and bake.

Rigodon de Basse Bourgogne
Ham and Pork Custard

1/2 pound sliced ham

1/2 pound cooked sliced pork

3 cups milk

salt to taste

6 eggs

1/3 cup flour

1 tablespoon butter

Layer meats in a buttered, 2-quart, ovenproof dish. Pour milk into a saucepan and season with salt. Bring to a boil. Lower heat. Beat eggs and flour together. Beat in milk and pour over meats. Dot with butter and bake in 350°F. oven until set.

Chapter 4

Omelets

Omelets are as popular on a brunch menu as, if not more so than, poached egg dishes. To the average customers, they represent the exotic and difficult—a chance for them to eat something they may not cook at home. Omelets can be filled with almost anything, as can crepes, and therefore lend themselves to great diversity.

It is the preference of the individual chef as to whether the omelet's exterior should be browned, as it often is in the United States, or the pale gold of the ideal French version. Omelets are

Omelette Benedict

1/2 cup diced lean ham
1/2 teaspoon butter
1/2 cup tiny fried croutons
3-egg omelet
 1 cup tarragon-flavored
  Mousseline sauce

Saute the ham in butter and add croutons. Fill omelet. Fold and coat with sauce. Glaze.

Brazilian Omelet

1/2 pound lean beef, ground
2 cups canned tomatoes
1 small green pepper, julienne
1 tablespoon minced green chilies
1 teaspoon chili powder
1/4 teaspoon salt
1/4 teaspoon sugar
4 3-egg omelets

Brown beef and drain off excess fat. Stir in tomatoes, pepper, chilies, chili powder, salt, and sugar. Prepare and fill omelets. Put on a plate and cut a lengthwise slit to expose filling.

usually folded around a filling; however, they may be folded and then split to expose the filling or they can be folded empty, split, and filled. Some omelets are made flat, like the Italian frittata.

Omelets lend variety to your offerings, and you can take advantage of the fact that they are traditionally a way of using leftovers. Remember to serve omelets immediately so that they are still light and fluffy when the guests receive them.

Omelette a l'Arlesienne

Omelet with Eggplant and Tomatoes

1 small eggplant, diced
  salt and pepper to taste
3 tablespoons oil
2 tomatoes, peeled, 1/2-inch slices
1 tablespoon butter
1/2 teaspoon minced garlic
3-egg omelet
1 teaspoon minced parsley

Salt eggplant; drain, rinse, and dry. Brown eggplant in oil and set aside. Cook tomatoes in butter with garlic for 2 minutes. Add eggplant and correct seasoning. Fill omelet and garnish top with eggplant mixture. Sprinkle with minced parsley.

L'Omelette du Baron du Barante

Lobster and Mushroom Omelet

1/2 pound mushrooms, sliced
4 tablespoons butter
  salt and pepper to taste
1/2 cup port
1/2 cup heavy cream
2 lobster tails, cooked, sliced
2 3-egg omelets
  grated Parmesan

Saute mushrooms in butter. Season with salt and pepper. Stir in port and cream and reduce by half. Add lobster and heat. Prepare omelets and fill with lobster mixture. Fold, sprinkle with Parmesan, and glaze.

Omelette Bourguignonne

Omelet with Snails

1/3 cup minced onion
1/3 cup minced shallots
2 tablespoons minced garlic
2 tablespoons butter
4 tablespoons flour
1 cup whole tinned tomatoes
4-1/2-ounce tin snails
1/4 cup carrots, diced, cooked
  salt and pepper to taste
2 3-egg omelets

Saute onion, shallots, and garlic in butter until tender. Stir in flour and cook over low heat until browned. Blend in tomatoes and 1/4 cup of liquid from snails. Add snails, carrots, salt, and pepper. Cook for 10 to 15 minutes. Prepare and fill omelets.

4 Omelets

Omelette Gargamelle
Omelet Gargamelle

2 cups minced mushrooms
3 scallions, minced
5 tablespoons dry vermouth
3/4 cup heavy cream
 salt and pepper to taste
1 teaspoon cornstarch
3 3-egg omelets
3 thin slices Gruyere
1 tablespoon grated Parmesan
 paprika

Simmer mushrooms, scallions, vermouth, and 1/2 cup cream for 5 minutes. Correct seasoning. Combine remaining cream with cornstarch and add to pan. Cook, stirring until thickened. Prepare omelet. Fill with half of the mixture and fold. Cover with remaining mixture. Top each omelet with Gruyere and sprinkle with Parmesan cheese and paprika. Glaze.

Omelette a la Choisy
Omelet with Creamed Lettuce

2 heads Boston lettuce, braised,
 minced
1 cup cream sauce
6 3-egg omelets

Combine lettuce with just enough sauce to bind. Prepare and fill omelets. Surround with a ribbon of cream sauce.

Princess Omelet

8 eggs

1/2 cup sour cream

4 teaspoons minced onion

pinch of cayenne pepper

1/2 teaspoon salt

6 ounces cream cheese, 1/4-inch cubes

butter

1 pound cooked asparagus

Combine eggs, sour cream, onion, pepper, and salt. Stir in cream cheese. Heat butter in a skillet and make four omelets. Fill with half of the asparagus and fold. Garnish with remaining asparagus.

Omelette Normande

1-1/2 pounds apples, peeled, cored, sliced

6 tablespoons butter

3 tablespoons calvados

3 3-egg omelets

pinch of salt

sugar

Saute apples in 3 tablespoons butter and 1 tablespoon calvados until tender. Combine eggs, salt, and pinch of sugar. Prepare omelets with remaining butter and fill with apples. Fold and turn onto heatproof platter. Sprinkle with sugar and glaze. Flame with remaining calvados.

Omelet with Ricotta and Salami

1/2 cup ricotta
1/2 cup diced Genoa salami
    salt and pepper to taste
3 3-egg omelets
    butter

Combine ricotta and salami. Season with salt and pepper. Prepare omelets and fill. Brush with butter. Slit to expose filling.

Omelette Savoyarde
Rolled Omelet with Potatoes and Cheese

1 cup sliced cooked potatoes
4 tablespoons butter
1/3 cup shredded Gruyere
1/4 cup heavy cream
    salt and pepper to taste
2 3-egg omelets
    minced parsley

Heat potatoes in butter. Stir in cheese, cream, salt, and pepper. Set aside. Prepare omelets and fill with potato mixture. Fold. Sprinkle with parsley.

Royal Omelet

2 ounces grated Parmesan
1 ounce butter
1 cup heavy cream
6 eggs, separated
3 tablespoons heavy cream
1 tablespoon grated Parmesan

Melt cheese in butter over low heat. Stir in cream and heat until it thickens. Do not boil. Set aside. Prepare fluffy omelets, cooking until firm. Fold onto hot plates, coat with sauce, and sprinkle with remaining cream and cheese. Glaze.

Frittata di Zucchini
Zucchini Flat Omelet

2 small zucchini, thinly sliced
   flour
3 tablespoons olive oil
6 eggs, lightly beaten
1 tablespoon grated Parmesan
   salt and pepper to taste
   pinch of ground thyme

Dredge zucchini in flour and cook in olive oil until tender. Combine eggs, cheese, salt, pepper, and thyme. Pour over zucchini and cook until set and browned on one side. Turn and brown the other side. Serve cut into wedges. Can be made in 5-inch pans for individual servings.

Omelette aux Noix
Walnut Omelet

8 eggs
  salt and pepper to taste
20 walnuts
  butter

Beat eggs with salt and pepper. Heat walnuts in butter until foamy. Pour in eggs and cook until set and lightly browned. Turn and lightly brown other side.

Omelette Ropa Vieja
Cuban "Old Clothes" Omelet

2 tomatoes, peeled, seeded, chopped
  butter
1/2 cup shredded chicken or ham
4 eggs, lightly beaten
1 tablespoon minced parsley

Heat tomatoes in butter. Add chicken or ham and heat. Add eggs and parsley. Cover and cook over low heat until set and lightly browned on the bottom. Fold and serve.

Omelette a la Savoyarde
Flat Savoy Omelet

2 medium potatoes, boiled, thinly sliced
7 tablespoons butter
8 eggs, lightly beaten
  salt and pepper to taste
1/4 cup grated Gruyere
1 teaspoon minced chervil

Brown potatoes in butter. Pour in eggs, salt, pepper, cheese, and chervil. Cook as a flat omelet and cut into wedges.

South American Omelet

1 large avocado, halved
8 eggs
salt and pepper to taste
1 tablespoon oil
2 tablespoons butter

Cut half of avocado into cubes, remainder into balls. Beat eggs with salt and pepper and add diced avocado. Cook in oil and butter for a flat omelet. Turn out and garnish with avocado balls.

La Piperade du Pays Basque
Basque Pepper Omelet

1 green pepper, sliced
1 tablespoon olive oil
4 tomatoes, peeled, seeded, chopped
1 onion, sliced
1/2 clove garlic, crushed
1/4 cup cooked, diced ham
salt and pepper to taste
2 tablespoons butter
4 eggs

Saute pepper in olive oil. Add tomatoes, onion, garlic, and ham. Correct seasoning. Add butter and simmer until tomatoes are a soft puree. Beat eggs with salt and pepper and add to vegetable mixture. Cook until barely set as a flat omelet. Should be soft.

4 *Omelets*

Chapter 5

Fried & Scrambled Eggs

Although it is common to serve fried and scrambled eggs without embellishment, there are a number of ways to enhance them and turn them from ordinary breakfast fare into exciting brunch dishes. This is particularly helpful for the foodservice that must cater to the same group of diners over extended periods, such as resorts.

Oeufs a l'Espagnole
Eggs Spanish Style

2 fried eggs
2 tomato halves, fried in oil
1/2 cup fried onion rings
4 tablespoons tomato sauce
1 teaspoon minced pimiento

Place eggs in center of plate, alternating with tomatoes. Fill center with onions. Pour a ring of tomato sauce mixed with pimiento around outside edge.

Oeufs a la Clementine
Eggs Clementine

4 slices toast, fried in butter
1/2 cup shredded Gruyere
1/4 cup dry white wine
salt and pepper to taste
4 fried eggs

Arrange toast in ovenproof serving dish. Melt cheese in saucepan with wine. Season with salt and pepper. Pour over bread. Top with eggs and reheat, if necessary.

Salisbury Steak with Fried Eggs

1 pound raw hamburger
1 tablespoon minced green
  pepper
1 tablespoon butter
1 tablespoon minced parsley
1 tablespoon minced onion
3 tablespoons bread crumbs
1 egg
  salt, pepper, nutmeg, and
  thyme to taste
6 slices toast
6 fried eggs
1-1/2 cups tomato sauce

Combine hamburger, pepper sauteed in butter, parsley, onion, bread crumbs, egg, salt, pepper, nutmeg, and thyme. Shape into 6 patties. Broil until medium. Place patties on toast. Top with egg and surround with tomato sauce.

Huevos Fritos a la Espagnola
Spanish Fried Eggs

1 large onion, chopped
4 tomatoes, peeled, chopped
3 green peppers, chopped
4 tablespoons olive oil
  salt and pepper to taste
4 fried eggs
8 toast points

Saute onion, tomatoes, and peppers in oil until softened. Correct seasoning. Cook to a thick puree. Place puree in warm serving dish. Top with fried eggs and garnish with toast triangles.

Scrambled Eggs in Tomato Cup

6 tomatoes, hollowed and drained
  salt and pepper to taste
12 eggs, scrambled
12 anchovy strips

Season tomato shells with salt and pepper and heat in the oven. Fill with eggs and top with anchovies.   40

Popovers with Scrambled Eggs

6 popovers

12 eggs, scrambled with chives

Cut popovers open and fill with eggs.

Uova alla Milano

Eggs Milan Style

3 tablespoons butter

1/4 pound grated Parmesan

1 tablespoon minced shallots

1 tablespoon minced chives

1 cup dry white wine

8 eggs, beaten with salt, pepper, and nutmeg

16 toast triangles

Melt butter. Stir in cheese, shallots, and chives. Slowly stir in wine and heat until smooth. Pour in eggs and cook slowly until just set; eggs should be loose. Serve on a warm platter. Garnish with toast triangles.

Uova alla Salsa di Gambero

Eggs with Shrimp Sauce

2 tablespoons butter

1 tablespoon olive oil

2 tablespoons minced onion

2 tablespoons minced parsley

5 ounces unshelled shrimp

salt to taste

1/2 ounce toasted, ground pine nuts

6 tablespoons hot water

6 fried eggs

12 sauteed shrimp in shells

In a saucepan melt butter. Add oil, onion, and parsley. Saute until tender. Add shrimp, salt, and pine nuts. Simmer 5 minutes longer. Add water and simmer 30 minutes. Puree in processor and force through a fine sieve. Reheat. Place eggs on a serving plate. Surround with sauce and garnish with sauteed shrimp.

Fried & 5 Scrambled Eggs

Scrambled Eggs and Smoked Salmon

4 tablespoons butter
1/2 cup minced onions
1/2 pound thinly sliced smoked salmon
12 eggs
   black pepper to taste
   minced parsley

Melt butter and cook onions until soft, but not brown. Add salmon and heat. Scramble eggs. Stir in salmon when just about set. Sprinkle with pepper and parsley.

Lox and Eggs

1 large onion, chopped
1 green pepper, chopped
2 cups sliced mushrooms
1/2 cup butter
1/2 pound smoked salmon, diced
8 eggs
1 tablespoon minced parsley
1/4 teaspoon dried basil
   dash of Tabasco
   salt and pepper to taste

In a skillet, saute the onion, pepper, and mushrooms in butter until soft. Add the salmon and cook until just heated. Beat eggs with parsley, basil, Tabasco, salt, and pepper. Add to salmon mixture and scramble. Serve hot.

Oeufs a la Parisienne
*Hard Cooked Eggs
Parisian
(See page 17.)*

Crepes aux Pommes
*Apple Crepes
(See page 70.)*

Huevos Fritos a
l'Espagnola
Spanish Fried Eggs
(See page 40.)

Oeufs Poches a la
Victoria
Poached Eggs Victoria
(See page 4.)

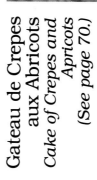

Sauce aux Moules
Safranee
*Saffron and Mussel
Sauce*
(See page 76.)

Gateau de Crepes
aux Abricots
*Cake of Crepes and
Apricots*
(See page 70.)

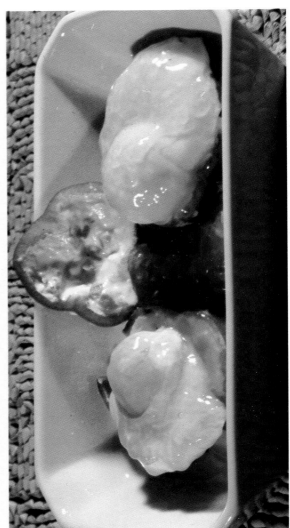

Oeufs Dur en Tapenade
Hard Cooked Eggs with
Olive-Anchovy Sauce
(See page 16.)

Oeufs Poches Louisiane
Cold Poached Eggs
Louisiana
(See page 6.)

Mushroom, Onion,
and Sausage Quiche
(See page 53.)

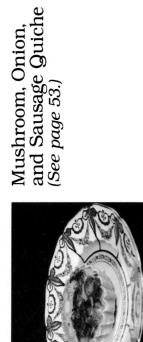

Omelette
Bourguignonne
Omelet with Snails
(See page 31.)

Clam Pie
(See page 50.)

Eggs and Oysters
(See page 12.)

Riz a la Dreux
Rice Molds
with Scrambled Eggs
and Kidneys
(See page 44.)

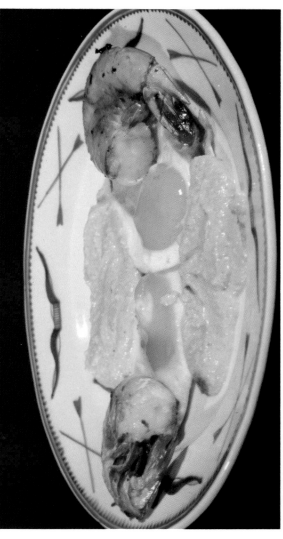

Crepes Nicoise
(See page 66.)

Truite Souffle
avec Sauce Mousseline
*Trout Souffle with
Mousseline Sauce
(See page 58.)*

Uova alla Salsa di
Gambero
*Eggs with Shrimp Sauce
(See page 41.)*

Color Plate 15

Oeufs Dur aux Olives
*Hard Cooked Eggs with
Olives*
(See page 11.)

**Seafood Crepes,
Brandy's**
(See page 65.)

Oeufs Offenbach

Scrambled Eggs with Shrimp

12 eggs, scrambled
3 anchovies, minced
3 ounces tuna fish, flaked
   salt and pepper to taste
6 slices buttered, hot toast
2 large tomatoes, peeled, seeded
12 medium shrimp, cooked, peeled
2 tablespoons minced parsley

Before eggs are set, stir in anchovies and tuna. Correct seasoning. Arrange toast on hot plates. Cut tomatoes into 6 1/4-inch thick slices and dice remainder. Place a tomato slice on each piece of toast. Top with eggs and garnish with shrimp, diced tomato, and minced parsley.

Scrambled Eggs with Snail Toasts

24 toast rectangles
  8 tablespoons garlic butter
24 snails
1/4 cup shredded Gruyere
12 eggs, scrambled with chives

Spread toast with half of butter. Top with snails, dot with remaining butter, and sprinkle with cheese. Heat in hot oven. Arrange eggs on serving plate and surround with snail toasts.

Riz a la Dreux

Rice Molds with Scrambled Eggs and Kidneys

2 veal kidneys, thinly sliced
3 tablespoons butter
2 tablespoons flour
3/4 cup hot chicken stock
1/4 cup Madeira
    salt, pepper, and nutmeg to taste
6 1/2-cup hot rice molds
12 eggs, scrambled

Saute veal kidneys in butter until lightly browned. Add flour and cook stirring for 2 minutes. Add stock and Madeira with seasonings. Simmer 10 minutes. Arrange rice molds on serving plates. Surround with scrambled eggs and garnish with kidneys.

Scrambled Eggs a la Caracas

8 ounces smoked dried beef, minced
3 cups tomatoes, peeled, seeded, chopped
3/4 cup grated Parmesan
1/4 cup minced onion
    pinch of cinnamon
    pinch of cayenne
6 tablespoons butter
9 eggs, well beaten

Saute the beef, tomatoes, cheese, onion, cinnamon, and cayenne in butter. Add eggs and scramble. Serve.

Sausage Cups with Chive Scrambled Eggs

1-1/2 pounds sausage meat
  1 tablespoon minced onion
  1 cup uncooked oats
  1 egg
1/4 cup milk
  12 eggs
  6 ounces cream cheese with chives, in small cubes

Combine sausage, onion, oats, egg, and milk. Press into muffin tins, forming into small cups. Bake at 325°F. for 30 minutes, or until cooked. Drain excess fat, unmold, and keep warm. Scramble eggs. When almost cooked, stir in cheese cubes. Serve in sausage cups.

Oeufs Brouilles a l'Alice

Scrambled Eggs Alice

  6 large cream puffs
  12 eggs, scrambled
  6 mushroom caps, sauteed in butter
  6 slices crisp bacon

Split puffs, fill with eggs, and garnish with bacon and mushroom caps.

Oeufs Brouilles Nicoise

Scrambled Eggs Nicoise

  2 cups eggplant mixture (see page 30)
  1 cup cubed slab bacon
  12 eggs, scrambled
  5 tablespoons parsley butter

Keep eggplant mixture warm. Cook bacon in heavy skillet until almost crisp. Stir into eggplant mixture. When eggs are cooked, stir in parsley butter. Arrange on a serving dish and surround with Provencale mixture.

Fried & Scrambled Eggs 5

Chapter 6

Quiches

Quiches are another item that will lure customers and profits to your establishment. Quiche ingredients are inexpensive and the variations infinite. Although these recipes are written for standard pie shells, these quiches also can be made in individual servings or in large sheet pans for larger institutions.

Quiche Lorraine

6 slices lean bacon, cooked
6 ounces grated, or thinly sliced, Emmenthaler or Gruyere
9-inch pie shell, half baked
4 large eggs
2 cups heavy cream
salt, pepper, and nutmeg to taste
butter

Preheat oven to 375°F. Arrange bacon and cheese in bottom of pie shell. Beat eggs with cream, salt, pepper, and nutmeg. Pour into shell. Bake 35 to 40 minutes.

Carrot Tart

2 pounds carrots, sliced
1/2 teaspoon sugar
1/2 teaspoon salt
1/3 cup butter
    pepper to taste
    dash of lemon juice
9-inch pie shell, baked
3 scallions, minced

Cover carrots with water and add sugar and salt. Simmer until water has been absorbed and carrots are tender. Set aside 1-1/2 cups carrots. Add butter to remaining carrots and mash. Season with pepper and lemon juice. Spread carrot puree in bottom of shell. Arrange reserved slices on top. Sprinkle with scallions. Reheat.

Asparagus Pie

2 cups heavy cream
1 large bay leaf
4 sprigs parsley
4 thin onion slices
    pinch of thyme
    pinch of marjoram
6 whole peppercorns
1 tablespoon butter
3 tablespoons lean minced ham
9-inch pie shell, baked
1 pound asparagus, cooked
1/2 cup grated Gruyere
3/4 cup fresh bread crumbs
    butter

Simmer cream, bay leaf, parsley, onion, thyme, marjoram, and peppercorns for 15 minutes. Heat ham in butter until hot. Strain cream into ham and simmer 30 minutes, or until reduced to 1 cup. Line pie shell with asparagus. Pour in just enough sauce to cover. Combine remaining sauce with cheese and pour over asparagus. Sprinkle with bread crumbs and dot with butter. Glaze under broiler.

Mexican Quiche with Chilies and Cheese

1 tablespoon minced shallots
2 tablespoons butter
4 ounces green chilies, minced
9-inch pie shell, baked blond
2 cups grated Cheddar
4 large eggs
1 cup heavy cream
1/2 teaspoon salt

Preheat oven to 350°F. Saute shallots in butter. Add chilies and put into pie shell. Sprinkle with cheese. Combine eggs and cream with salt and pour into shell. Bake until set.

Quiche with Anchovy or Crabmeat, Dit a l'Intrigue

4 large eggs, lightly beaten
1 cup cream
   salt and pepper to taste
9-inch pie shell, baked blond
2 ounces anchovy fillets, or
4 ounces crabmeat
3/4 cup grated Parmesan
1 tablespoon minced onion

Beat eggs, cream, salt, and pepper. Pour 1/3 of mixture into pie shell. Bake at 400°F. for 5 minutes. Arrange anchovies or crabmeat over egg and spoon on another 1/3 of egg. Bake 5 minutes or until just set. Sprinkle with cheese and onions. Spoon on remaining egg. Bake 20 minutes until puffed and browned.

Quiche Honfleuraise

Seafood Quiche

3 pounds mussels, scrubbed and
    bearded
2 shallots, minced
2 onions, minced
3/4 cup white wine
    salt and pepper to taste
1/2 pint oysters
1/4 pound shrimp, shelled
    9-inch pie shell, half baked
1 cup heavy cream
3 eggs, lightly beaten
    nutmeg to taste

Cook mussels with shallots, onions, wine, salt, and pepper. Strain and reserve liquid. Remove mussels from shells and reserve. Poach oysters and drain. Cook shrimp in strained mussel liquor. Save liquid. Place mussels, oysters, and shrimp in bottom of shell. Beat cream, eggs, salt, pepper, and nutmeg. Pour into shell and bake at 425°F. for 30 minutes.

Clam Pie

    pastry for 2-crust, 9-inch pie
1 tablespoon minced parsley
1/4 cup minced onion
3 tablespoons butter
3 tablespoons flour
1 cup heavy cream
1/2 cup clam juice
1 cup minced clams

Line a pie plate with pastry and sprinkle with parsley. Saute onion in butter until soft. Add flour and cook roux. Add cream and clam juice and bring to a boil. Spread a layer of clams in shell and add some sauce. Continue until ingredients have been used. Top with pastry cover. Brush with dorure. Bake for 40 minutes at 425°F.

Quiche au Homard

Lobster Quiche

1 unbaked pie shell
1 egg white, lightly beaten
2 tablespoons minced shallots
1-1/2 tablespoons butter
1/2 pound cooked lobster meat, diced
2 tablespoons cognac
1/2 teaspoon dried tarragon
2 cups heavy cream, heated
4 eggs, well beaten
1 teaspoon minced chives
1 truffle, optional
   salt and pepper to taste
4 drops Tabasco

Preheat oven to 425° F. Brush pie shell with egg white and bake 5 minutes. Saute shallots in butter until soft. Stir in lobster. Heat and sprinkle with cognac and tarragon. Blend cream and eggs with chives, truffle, salt, pepper, and Tabasco. Add to lobster mixture and pour into shell. Bake 15 minutes. Lower heat to 350°F. and bake 10 minutes, or until cooked.

Salmon Quiche

2 tablespoons minced shallots
2 tablespoons butter
1 pound salmon, poached, skinned, boned, and flaked
3 tablespoons minced dill
   salt and pepper to taste
1/4 cup liquid from poaching salmon
   9-inch pie shell, half baked
1 cup heavy cream
4 eggs, lightly beaten
   tomato rose

Preheat oven to 375°F. Saute shallots in butter. Combine with salmon, dill, salt, pepper, and poaching liquor. Pour into shell. Combine cream and eggs and correct seasoning. Pour into shell and bake until set, about 30 minutes. Garnish with tomato rose.

6 *guiches*

Italian Quiche

6 eggs
1 cup milk
7 ounces tuna in oil, drained, flaked
1/2 pound grated Mozzarella
  salt and pepper to taste
1/2 teaspoon each, dried basil and dried oregano
  9-inch pie shell, unbaked

Beat eggs and milk until blended. Stir in tuna, cheese, and seasonings. Pour into shell and bake at 375°F. until set.

Beef and Tomato Quiche

1 bunch scallions, sliced
1 pound lean ground beef
2 tablespoons butter
1 large tomato, peeled, seeded, chopped
1-1/4 teaspoons salt
1/2 teaspoon marjoram
1/2 teaspoon thyme
1/2 teaspoon pepper
1-1/4 cups heavy cream
4 eggs, lightly beaten
  9-inch pie shell, half baked
1 tablespoon minced parsley

Preheat oven to 375°F. Saute scallions and beef in butter until beef loses its color. Stir in tomato, salt, marjoram, thyme, and pepper. Cook until flavors blend. Add cream to eggs. Add meat to egg mixture. Pour into pie shell and bake until set, about 30 minutes. Sprinkle with parsley.

Mushroom, Onion, and Sausage Quiche

1/2 pound sliced onions
2 tablespoons bacon fat
2 eggs
2 egg yolks
2 teaspoons Dijon mustard
1/2 cup grated Parmesan
1-1/4 cups light cream
1/2 pound sliced mushrooms
2 tablespoons butter
1 tablespoon lemon juice
   salt and pepper to taste
1/2 pound sausage meat, cooked and crumbled
9-inch pie shell, half baked

Preheat oven to 350°F. Saute onion in bacon fat. Beat eggs, egg yolks, mustard, and Parmesan and add to onions with cream. Saute mushrooms in butter and lemon juice. Correct seasoning. Combine sausage, onion mixture, and mushrooms. Pour into shell and bake about 30 minutes.

Artichoke and Sausage Quiche

1/2 cup minced scallions
1 tablespoon butter
10 ounces cooked artichoke hearts
4 eggs
1 pound Ricotta
1/2 cup sour cream
2 ounces grated Parmesan
4 ounces grated Gruyere
3 ounces ham, julienne
1/3 cup minced parsley
3/4 pound mild Italian sausage, cooked, peeled, thinly sliced
   salt and pepper to taste
10-inch springform pan, lined with pie pastry

Preheat oven to 425°F. Saute scallions in butter. Add artichokes and heat. Beat eggs with Ricotta and sour cream until well blended. Stir in Parmesan, Gruyere, ham, parsley, sausage, scallions, and artichokes. Correct seasoning. Pour into prepared pastry. Bake 10 minutes. Lower heat to 375°F. and bake for 20 minutes.

6 quiches

Zucchini and Ham Quiche

1/4 cup minced onion
1 small clove garlic, minced
2 tablespoons butter
    salt and pepper to taste
1-1/4 pounds zucchini, thinly sliced
1/4 pound sliced boiled ham,
    finely diced
4 large eggs
3/4 cup milk
1/2 cup heavy cream
1/4 cup grated Parmesan
9-inch pie shell, half baked

Preheat oven to 375°F. Saute onion and garlic in butter until soft but not brown. Add salt, pepper, and zucchini and cook until tender. Add ham and stir to blend. Beat eggs, milk, and cream together. Correct seasoning. Combine with zucchini mixture and Parmesan. Pour into pie shell and bake about 30 minutes.

Chapter 7

Soufflés

To keep in tune with current tastes and the craving for light foods, it is worth considering the soufflé. The soufflé is, of course, a high profit dessert, but it can be equally profitable on the brunch menu. Although soufflés must be served immediately after baking, they can be assembled and refrigerated for several hours before baking. Put them in a preheated 400° F. oven and they will be ready to serve in a few minutes, if made in individual servings. Once again, it is possible to appear lavish with expensive ingredients, since soufflés use only small amounts.

Soufflé au Fromage
Cheese Soufflé

3 tablespoons butter
3 tablespoons flour
1-1/2 cups hot milk
1/2 teaspoon salt
   pinch of cayenne
   pinch of grated nutmeg
4 egg yolks
3/4–1 cup grated Gruyere, Parmesan, or cheddar
5 egg whites

Preheat oven to 375° F. Butter a 1-quart soufflé dish or four 1-cup ramekins. Dust inside with bread crumbs. Make sauce with butter, flour, milk, salt, cayenne, and nutmeg. Beat in egg yolks and cook to form liaison. Stir in cheese until melted. Cool. Beat egg whites until stiff and fold into cheese mixture. Pour into prepared soufflé dishes. Bake.

Souffle de Gourilos

Escarole Souffle

3 tablespoons butter

3 scallions, thinly sliced

1 head escarole, shredded, blanched

1/2 teaspoon Worcestershire

1 recipe cheese souffle with cheddar (see page 55)

Saute scallions in butter. Add escarole and cook until the liquid has evaporated. Fold into the souffle mixture. Add Worcestershire before adding egg whites.

Muenster and Caraway Souffle

1 recipe cheese souffle (see page 55)

Substitute 1 cup diced Muenster for another cheese. Fold in 1-1/2 teaspoons caraway seeds. Bake.

Souffle au Fromage aux Croutons d'Ail

Cheese Souffle with Garlic Croutons

1 recipe cheese souffle with Gruyere (see page 55)

1 cup croutons sauteed in garlic butter

2 cups tomato sauce

Fold croutons into souffle mixture before folding in egg whites. Fill molds and bake. Serve with sauce on the side.

lobster meat from shells and cut into 1/4-inch slices. Reduce cooking liquid by 1/2. Add cream sauce, remaining cream, and sherry. Strain. Pour 1/2 of sauce over lobster. Place in the bottom of a souffle dish. Prepare souffle and put on top of lobster. Bake. Serve remaining sauce on the side.

Souffle de Homard

Lobster Souffle

- 1   1-3/4-pound lobster
- 1   tablespoon butter
- 2   tablespoons mirepoix
- 1/2 tablespoon minced chives
- 1/2 tablespoon minced parsley
  salt and pepper to taste
- 1/4 cup vegetable oil
- 1/2 teaspoon paprika
- 1   tablespoon cognac
- 1/4 cup dry white wine
- 1/2 cup plus 1-1/2 tablespoons heavy cream
- 1/2 cup cream sauce
- 1-1/2 tablespoons dry sherry
- 1   recipe cheese souffle, made with half Parmesan and half Gruyere (see page 55)

Remove lobster claws and tails and cut into 3 pieces. Saute mirepoix in butter until soft. Season with chives, parsley, and salt and pepper. Heat oil in a skillet. Add lobster, mirepoix, and paprika and cook until lobster turns red. Flame with cognac. Add wine and 1/2 cup heavy cream. Simmer 10 minutes. Remove from heat. Remove

Salmon and Broccoli Souffle

1 recipe cheese souffle using 4 tablespoons Parmesan (see page 55)

1/2 cup cooked, flaked salmon

1-1/2 teaspoons tomato paste

1 teaspoon minced fresh dill

10 ounces broccoli, pureed

1/4 teaspoon nutmeg

2 tablespoons grated Parmesan

Preheat oven to 400°F. Before folding in egg whites, divide souffle mixture into 2 parts. Combine salmon, tomato paste, dill, and half of souffle mixture. Combine broccoli, nutmeg, and remaining sauce base. Beat egg whites until stiff and fold 1/2 into salmon mixture and 1/2 into broccoli mixture. Fill souffle dish first with broccoli then with salmon mixture. Sprinkle top with remaining Parmesan. Bake.

Truite Souffle Avec Sauce Mousseline

Trout Souffle with Mousseline Sauce

1 pound poached trout, skinned, boned

1 recipe cheese souffle with Gruyere

2 tablespoons grated Parmesan

2 cups Mousseline sauce

Preheat oven to 375°F. Puree half the fish and fold into souffle base before adding whites. Add whites. Spoon 1/2 of mixture into souffle dish and top with slices of trout. Top with remaining souffle mixture. Sprinkle top with Parmesan. Bake. Serve with sauce on the side.

Omelette Normande
(See page 33.)

Broiled Marinated
Scallops
(See page 78.)

Omelette a la Choisy
Omelet with Creamed
Lettuce
(See page 32.)

Baked Haddock
Cottage Style
(See page 79.)

Oeufs Offenbach
Scrambled Eggs with
Shrimp
(See page 43.)

Oeufs Brouilles
Nicoise
Scrambled Eggs Nicoise
(See page 45.)

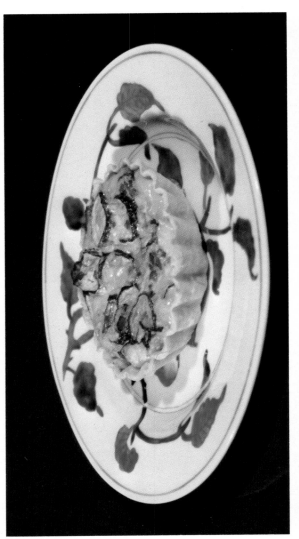

Zucchini and Ham
Quiche
(See page 54.)

Chicken, Broccoli,
and Noodle Casserole
(See page 85.)

Oeufs Poches Aurore
Poached Eggs Aurora
(See page 4.)

**La Piperade du Pays
Basque**
Basque Pepper Omelet
(See page 37.)

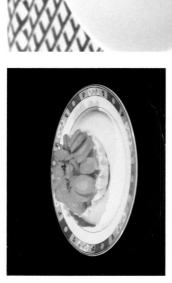

Carrot Tart
(See page 48.)

Creamed Beef and
Sausage over
Curried Noodles
(See page 92.)

Espadon en
Brochettes
Swordfish on Skewers
(See page 81.)

Oeufs sur le Plat Lully
Shirred Eggs Lully
(See page 23.)

Baked Eggs Deerfoot
(See page 21.)

Oeufs Farcis au
Cognac
*Hard Cooked Eggs with
Cognac-Olive Sauce*
(See page 17.)

Oysters Astor
(See page 76.)

Oeufs a l'Espagnole
Eggs Spanish Style
(See page 39.)

Souffles aux Crevettes a l'Estragon

Shrimp Souffle with Tarragon

- 4 tablespoons butter
- 2 tablespoons minced onion
- 1 tablespoon minced shallot
- 1 teaspoon minced garlic
- 2 cups tomatoes, peeled, seeded, chopped
- salt and pepper to taste
- 1-1/2 tablespoons tarragon
- 1 tablespoon minced parsley
- 1/3 cup dry white wine
- 1 pound shrimp, peeled
- cayenne pepper to taste
- 2 tablespoons cognac
- 1 recipe cheese souffle made with half Gruyere and half Parmesan

Preheat oven to 375°F. Saute onion and shallot with garlic in 2 tablespoons butter until soft. Add tomatoes, salt, pepper, tarragon, and parsley and simmer 5 minutes. Add wine and simmer 15 minutes. Saute shrimp in remaining butter with cayenne. Correct seasoning and flame with cognac. Add tomato mixture and correct seasoning. Place in bottom of souffle dish. Top with souffle mixture and bake. For individual servings, prepare in small ramekins. For groups of six, shape souffle in jelly roll pan. Bake roll, fill with sauce mixture, and serve cut into slices.

Souffle au Fromage et Jambon

Cheese and Ham Souffle

- 1 recipe cheese souffle with Gruyere
- 1 cup finely diced ham
- 2 tablespoons Dijon mustard

Prepare souffle mixture except for folding in egg whites. Fold the ham and mustard into the sauce base. Fold in the egg whites. Bake.

7 Souffles

Chapter 8

Crepes

One of the most popular dishes over the last twenty years has been the crepe. It has become a favorite of both the eating public and the cooking profession. Crepes can be filled with almost any mixture and thus are a good way of using leftovers and of using fresh ingredients while still keeping food costs low.

Crepes can be assembled in several different ways. Traditionally, the filling is placed on the crepe. It is then rolled, coated with a sauce, and glazed. Crepes can be filled with one of the souffle recipes from the previous chapter, folded into quarters,

Gateau de Crepes aux Champignons

Cake of Mushroom-Filled Crepes

12	6-inch crepes
1-1/2 cups	duxelles sauce
2 cups	grated Gruyere
2-1/2 cups	Bechamel sauce
1/2 cup	heavy cream

Place a crepe on an ovenproof serving platter. Cover with a layer of duxelles and top with another crepe. Combine Gruyere with Bechamel sauce. Spread on crepe. Keep layering, finishing with a crepe. Combine remaining Bechamel with heavy cream. Pour over the top of the cake. Bake at 425°F. for 10 minutes.

Mushroom and Watercress Crepes

2 pounds mushrooms, thinly
    sliced

1/2 cup butter
1/2 cup minced onion
1/2 teaspoon salt
2 tablespoons flour
1/2 cup dry white wine
2 cups sour cream
3 cups watercress leaves
1/2 teaspoon Worcestershire
16 entree crepes

Saute mushrooms in butter with onion and salt. Stir in flour and cook roux. Add wine and cook until thickened. Remove from heat. Stir in sour cream, watercress, and Worcestershire. Correct seasoning. Fill crepes, roll, and place in buttered baking dish. Reheat.

and baked in a 425°F. oven until puffed. They may also be assembled in layers with filling placed between like a layer cake. The cake can then be reheated and sauced. If the crepes are tiny, they can be assembled as individual cakes. If they are larger, they should be cut into wedges.

Spinach and Dill Crepes

1/2 cup minced scallions
3/4 cup butter
2 pounds spinach, cooked, minced
2 tablespoons minced dill
1 large clove garlic, crushed
1 cup sour cream
14 entree crepes, flavored with 1 tablespoon dill
3 tablespoons grated Parmesan
2 cups sour cream, optional

Saute scallions in 4 tablespoons butter. Add spinach and correct seasoning. Stir in dill, garlic, and 3 tablespoons sour cream. Cook until liquid has evaporated. Fold in remainder of the cup of sour cream. Melt remaining butter. Preheat oven to 325°F. Fill crepes and roll. Arrange in baking dish and spoon on melted butter. Dust with cheese. Heat. Serve remaining sour cream on side, if desired.

Crespolini
Italian Crepes

1 pound spinach, cooked, minced
1 cup ricotta
2 eggs, lightly beaten
1/2 cup grated Parmesan
16 crepes
1 cup thin cream sauce
1 cup grated Muenster

Combine spinach, ricotta, eggs, and Parmesan. Fill crepes. Roll and place in ovenproof dish. Cover with cream sauce. Sprinkle with cheese and bake until bubbling. Glaze.

8 Crepes

Crepes Farcis a la Monegasque

Crepes Stuffed Monaco Style

3/4 cup butter

4 anchovy fillets, minced

3 tablespoons olive oil

2 cups thinly sliced onions

2 cloves garlic, minced

4–6 tomatoes, peeled, seeded, chopped

1 teaspoon oregano

salt and pepper to taste

6 pimiento-stuffed olives, thinly sliced

6 ripe olives, pitted, halved

1 cup minced pimiento

3/4 pound cooked shrimp, diced

16 crepes

Heat butter and anchovies until anchovies are dissolved and reserve. Saute onion and garlic in oil until lightly browned. Add tomatoes, oregano, salt, and pepper. Simmer until thickened. Add olives, pimientos, and shrimp and heat. Correct seasoning. Fill crepes. Drizzle anchovy butter over crepes before heating.

Cold Crepes with Smoked Salmon

8 ounces cream cheese, softened

1 cup sour cream

2 tablespoons minced dill

salt and pepper to taste

1/4 pound minced, smoked salmon

12–16 entree crepes made with dill

1 cup melted butter

Combine cream cheese, sour cream, dill, salt, pepper, and salmon. Correct seasoning. Fill each crepe with mixture and fold into triangles. Drizzle butter over and serve.

Seafood Crepes, Brandy's

2 cups dry white wine
2 cups water
1/2 cup chopped mushroom stems
1/4 cup minced onion
1 bay leaf
2 teaspoons cognac
1/2 pound shrimp, peeled
1/2 pound scallops
1/2 pound king crab, bite-size pieces
3 tablespoons butter
3 tablespoons flour
salt and pepper to taste
1 cup heavy cream
16 crepes

Combine wine, water, mushrooms, onion, bay leaf, and cognac. Reduce to 2 cups and strain. Poach shrimp and scallops in court bouillon. Strain and reserve liquid. Add crab to fish and keep warm. Make roux, add poaching liquor, and correct seasoning. Cook until thickened and smooth. Add cream and reduce to coating consistency. Bind fish with half of sauce. Fill crepes, roll, and top with remaining sauce. Glaze.

Crepes His Royal Highness Prince Bertil

1 pound cooked medium shrimp
1/4 cup minced dill
3/4 cup Hollandaise sauce
salt and pepper to taste
16 entree crepes
8 tablespoons melted butter
4 tablespoons Parmesan

Combine shrimp, dill, and Hollandaise. Correct seasoning. Fill crepes. Drizzle with butter and cheese. Glaze.

8 Crepes

Curried Chicken with Chutney Crepes

3/4 cup butter
2 cups minced onions
1/2 cup minced carrots
1/2 cup minced celery
1 apple, chopped
3-4 tablespoons curry powder
3 tablespoons flour
2 cups chicken stock
1 cup light cream
1 cup unsweetened coconut milk
2 cups poached chicken, cubed
1/4 cup minced mango chutney
16 crepes

Melt butter and saute onions, carrots, celery, and apple until soft. Stir in curry powder and flour and cook 2 minutes. Stir in chicken stock and simmer 15 minutes. Add cream and coconut milk and cook 5 minutes. Sieve. Combine half the sauce with chicken and chutney. Fill crepes. Spoon remaining sauce over top. Heat.

Crepes Nicoise

1 cup ground lean veal
1 cup ground lean pork
1/4 cup minced shallots
1 tablespoon minced parsley
    dash of cayenne
    salt and pepper to taste
3 tablespoons butter
3/4 cup heavy cream
1 tablespoon flour
12 entree crepes
1 cup thinly sliced mushrooms
    juice of 1 lemon
2 cups Bechamel sauce
    grated Parmesan or Gruyere

Combine veal, pork, shallots, parsley, cayenne, salt, and pepper. Saute in 2 tablespoons butter until mixture starts to brown. Stir in cream. Make beurre manie with remaining butter and 1 tablespoon flour, and thicken sauce. Fill crepes. Combine mushrooms and lemon juice in a saucepan with water to cover. Simmer 10 minutes. Strain and add mushrooms to sauce. Pour over crepes and sprinkle with cheese. Glaze.

Crepes Farcis a la Bernoise

Stuffed Crepes Bern Style

2 cups cubed slab bacon, blanched
8 leeks, sliced
  salt and pepper to taste
2 tablespoons minced parsley
1/2 teaspoon thyme
3 hard cooked eggs, minced
14 crepes
3/4 cup butter
1/2 cup grated Parmesan

Saute bacon until crisp. Remove. In 3 tablespoons bacon fat, sweat leeks until very tender. Season with salt and pepper. Add parsley, thyme, bacon, and eggs. Heat. Fill crepes and arrange in baking dish. Drizzle with butter and sprinkle with cheese. Heat.

Crepes au Jambon et Fromage

Ham and Cheese Crepes

16 slices ham
16 slices Gruyere
16 crepes
1/4 cup cognac
4 cups Bechamel sauce
  salt and pepper to taste
  grated Parmesan
  paprika

Roll slices of ham and cheese in crepes and put in casserole. Combine cognac and Bechamel and simmer 5 minutes. Correct seasoning. Pour over crepes and sprinkle with cheese and paprika. Heat.

Crepes Favorites

2 sweet red peppers, diced
1 pound sweetbreads, blanched, diced
1/2 cup prosciutto, diced
1/2 cup plus 4 tablespoons butter
2 cups chicken veloute
salt, pepper, and lemon juice to taste
16 crepes
grated Parmesan

Saute the pepper, sweetbreads, and ham in 4 tablespoons butter. Add veloute and simmer 5 minutes. Correct seasoning with salt, pepper, and lemon juice. Fill crepes, roll, and arrange in baking dish. Melt remaining butter. Pour on crepes, and sprinkle with cheese. Reheat.

Crepazes

1 cup heavy cream
salt and pepper to taste
10 6-inch crepes
6 ounces thinly sliced prosciutto or Westphalian ham
6 ounces thinly sliced Virginia ham
2 ounces grated Gruyere

Heat cream with salt and pepper. Lightly butter a charlotte mold or cake tin, 6 inches in diameter. Place a crepe in the bottom and top with a slice of ham and a tablespoon of cream. Keep layering, alternating ham slices as you proceed. Top layer should be a crepe. Heat. Unmold, sprinkle with cheese, and glaze. Serve cut into wedges.

zucchini and cook 5 minutes. Line each crepe with prosciutto, fill with vegetable mixture, and roll. Drizzle with butter and sprinkle with cheese. Reheat.

Curried Crab Crepes

1 apple, peeled, cored, sliced
4 shallots, minced
1/2 cup butter
    curry powder to taste
2 teaspoons crushed coriander
2 tablespoons flour
4 tablespoons milk
2 cups Bechamel sauce
    lemon juice to taste
    salt and pepper to taste
1 pound cooked crabmeat
5 tablespoons butter
5 tablespoons grated Parmesan
20 crepes

Saute apple and shallots in butter until soft. Stir in curry powder, coriander, and flour. Mix well and cook 5 minutes. Stir in milk to make a thick paste. Stir in Bechamel, lemon juice, salt, and pepper. Fold in crabmeat. Fill crepes and place in buttered baking dish. Dot with butter and a little grated Parmesan. Glaze.

Crepes Farcis Provencale

Crepes with Provencale Filling

3/4 cup olive oil
1 large eggplant, cubed
2 zucchini, diced
2 onions, thinly sliced
1 green pepper, thinly sliced
1 red pepper, thinly sliced
4 tomatoes, peeled, seeded, chopped
1 teaspoon dried basil
1/2 teaspoon dried oregano
2 tablespoons minced parsley
2 cloves garlic, minced
    salt and pepper to taste
16 entree crepes
16 slices prosciutto
3/4 cup melted butter
1/2 cup grated Parmesan

Saute eggplant in 1/2 cup olive oil. Remove. Saute zucchini in remaining oil until browned. Add onions, peppers, and tomatoes to skillet. Simmer until juices have evaporated. Season with basil, oregano, parsley, garlic, salt, and pepper. Add eggplant and

8 *Crepes*

Crepes aux Pommes

Apple Crepes

3 apples, peeled, cored, diced
6 tablespoons butter
juice of 1/2 lemon
5 tablespoons each apricot jam, chopped almonds
1/2 cup heavy cream, whipped
4 tablespoons calvados
12–16 dessert crepes
1/2 cup crushed macaroons
2–3 tablespoons sugar

Saute apples in 5 tablespoons butter and lemon juice until tender. Stir in apricot jam and almonds. Cool. Fold in cream flavored with apple jack. Fill crepes and fold into quarters. Put into baking dish, sprinkle with macaroons and sugar, and dot with remaining butter. Glaze.

Gateau de Crepes aux Abricots

Cake of Crepes and Apricots

1-1/2 cups stewed dried apricots
2 tablespoons rum
sugar to taste
12 dessert crepes
1 cup sour cream

Combine apricots with rum and sugar. Fill crepes by spreading with a thin layer of the mixture and stacking. Cover and heat at 350°F. Serve with sour cream on the side.

Although dessert is not usually part of a brunch, sweet crepes may be well received by your customers. Many people like to start their day with something sweet.

Crepes Nectarines

6 sliced nectarines

3 tablespoons grenadine

3 tablespoons cointreau

16 dessert crepes

4 tablespoons crushed macaroons

Marinate nectarines in grenadine and cointreau for 15 minutes. Fill crepes with nectarines and sprinkle with macaroons. Pour remaining marinade on top. Glaze.

Crepes aux Fraises

Strawberry Crepes

1/2 pint strawberries, sliced

1/4 cup sugar

3 tablespoons butter

2 tablespoons orange liqueur

1/2 cup heavy cream

12 dessert crepes

3 tablespoons sugar

Toss strawberries with 1/4 cup sugar. Melt butter and saute strawberries and sugar until it begins to caramelize. Add liqueur and cream. Cook until reduced by one-quarter. Fill crepes. Pour any juices over crepes and sprinkle with sugar. Glaze.

Chapter 9

Fish Dishes

Numerous fish dishes served at other meals work well at brunch. Many of the dishes can be composed of previously cooked fish or created from freshly cooked fish. Remember that previously cooked fish also can be used as a filling for omelets and crepes, or in a souffle.

Baked Avocado with Crab Aurore

4 tablespoons tomato puree
2 tablespoons grated onion
2 tablespoons butter
2 tablespoons curry powder
2 cups Bechamel sauce
1 pound cooked crabmeat
3 ripe avocados, peeled
salt to taste
juice of 1 lemon

Combine tomato puree, onion, butter, curry powder, Bechamel, and crabmeat. Heat. Halve avocados, remove pits, score flesh, and season with salt and lemon juice. Fill with crab mixture. Arrange in a baking dish. Add 1 inch boiling water. Cover and bake 20 minutes, or until tender.

Crabe a la Diable
Devilled Crab

2 cups crabmeat
2 tablespoons butter
2 cups Mornay sauce
1 teaspoon dry mustard
1/2 cup heavy cream
   grated Parmesan

Heat crabmeat in butter. Stir in 1 cup Mornay and mustard dissolved in water. Correct seasoning. Fill scallop shells or ramekins with crabmeat. Combine cream and remaining Mornay and coat the crabmeat Sprinkle with Parmesan and glaze.

Crabmeat Tetrazzini

1 teaspoon minced shallots
2 tablespoons butter
1/2 pound crabmeat
1 teaspoon paprika
1 cup cream sauce
   sherry to taste
1 egg yolk
1 pound thin spaghetti, cooked

Saute shallots in butter until soft, stir in crab, and heat. Stir in paprika. Bring cream sauce to a boil. Stir in sherry and incorporate the egg yolk. Combine sauce and crabmeat mixture. Serve over spaghetti.

Clam Hash

2 cups clams, finely minced
3 tablespoons butter
2 teaspoons minced parsley
1 teaspoon minced chives
    fine bread crumbs
2 tablespoons dry sherry
    salt and paprika to taste
    buttered toast

Heat clams in their juice with the butter. Add parsley and chives and bring to a simmer. Add enough bread crumbs to thicken. Season with sherry, salt, and paprika. Serve on buttered toast.

Moules a la Moutarde

Mussels in Mustard Cream Sauce

4 tablespoons butter
4 tablespoons minced shallots
1 teaspoon minced garlic
2 quarts mussels, scrubbed, bearded
    pepper to taste
1 cup heavy cream
2 tablespoons Dijon mustard

Heat butter. Add shallots, garlic, mussels, and pepper. Bring to a simmer, add cream, and cook covered until mussels start to open. Uncover and stir once or twice until the mussels have opened. Transfer mussels to soup bowls. Stir the mustard into the sauce and strain over the mussels.

Sauce aux Moules Safranee

Saffron and Mussel Sauce

5 tablespoons minced shallots
3 cups heavy cream
1 teaspoon minced saffron
  salt and pepper to taste
1 quart mussels, scrubbed, bearded
  pasta or poached fish

Combine shallots, cream, saffron, salt, and pepper. Simmer 10 minutes. Add mussels and cook until they open. Remove mussels from their shells and set aside. Reduce the sauce until thick enough to coat the back of a spoon. Return mussels to the sauce. Serve over cooked pasta or poached fish. Mussels and sauce may be served in soup bowls with French bread.

Oysters Astor

1 pint oysters
1 teaspoon minced shallots
1 tablespoon minced red pepper
2 tablespoons butter
2 tablespoons flour
1-1/2 teaspoons lemon juice
1-1/2 teaspoons vinegar
1 teaspoon Worcestershire
1/2 teaspoon glace de viande, or
  beef extract
  salt and paprika to taste
  sauteed bread slices
  cucumber pickles

Poach oysters, drain, and add enough water to the poaching liquor to make one cup. Saute shallot and pepper in butter until soft. Add flour and cook roux. Add oyster liquor, lemon juice, vinegar, Worcestershire, beef extract, salt, and paprika. Simmer until thickened and smooth. Arrange oysters on bread. Coat with sauce and garnish with thin cucumber pickle slices.

Scalloped Oysters

1 cup cracker crumbs
1/2 cup stale bread crumbs
1/2 cup melted butter
1 pint oysters
  salt and pepper to taste
  pinch of nutmeg
4 tablespoons oyster liquor
2 tablespoons cream

Preheat oven to 400°F. Combine cracker and bread crumbs. Stir in butter and place a thin layer in the bottom of a shallow casserole. Cover with a layer of oysters. Sprinkle with salt, pepper, and nutmeg. Add half of oyster liquor and cream. Repeat another layer of crumbs, oysters, liquor, and cream. Top with a final layer of crumbs. Bake 30 minutes.

Oyster Pie

1/3 pound sour cream pastry dough
4 slices bacon
1/4 cup minced onions
1/2 cup minced scallions
1/4 cup minced parsley
1/2 teaspoon cayenne
1 quart oysters, drained

Preheat oven to 400°F. Prepare dough and set aside. Cook bacon until crisp. Remove and drain. Saute onion in bacon fat until soft. Turn into a bowl and add bacon bits, scallions, parsley, and cayenne. Mix. Add oysters and combine. Butter 8 ramekins and add oyster filling. Roll dough into circles 1/3-inch thick. Place over edges of bowls, crimp edges, and score top. Brush with dorure. Bake 25 to 30 minutes or until dough is puffed and browned.

Broiled Marinated Scallops

2 pounds scallops
1 cup olive oil
1 cup dry white wine
1 clove garlic, minced
1 teaspoon tarragon
  salt and pepper to taste
1/2 cup minced parsley

Rinse scallops and drain. Combine olive oil, wine, garlic, tarragon, salt, pepper, and parsley. Add scallops and marinate 2 hours. Skewer and broil until done. Serve with lemon wedges.

Coquilles St. Jacques au Gratin

Scallops with Mushroom Duxelles

2 cups white wine court bouillon
2 pounds scallops
  salt and pepper to taste
1 pound sliced mushrooms
4 tablespoons butter
2 cups duxelles sauce
1 cup buttered bread crumbs
  minced parsley
  lemon wedges

Poach scallops in court bouillon. Drain and slice thickly. Season with salt and pepper. Saute mushrooms in butter. Combine mushrooms and scallops. Place in individual serving dishes and coat with duxelles sauce. Sprinkle with crumbs. Glaze. Sprinkle with parsley and garnish with lemon wedges.

Spinach Noodles with Scallops Provencale

1 pint scallops
1/4 cup milk
1-1/2 pounds tomatoes, peeled, seeded, chopped
1 bay leaf
salt and pepper to taste
3/4 cup flour
1/2 cup vegetable oil
1 tablespoon minced garlic
3 tablespoons butter
1/2 pound spinach noodles, cooked
2 tablespoons minced parsley

Put scallops in a bowl with milk. Heat tomatoes in a skillet. Set a sieve over a bowl and pour in tomatoes. Drain. Reduce drained juices by half. Add tomato pulp with bay leaf, salt, and pepper. Drain scallops, toss in flour, and saute in hot oil. Combine scallops and tomato sauce. Saute garlic in butter until golden. Combine noodles, garlic, scallops, and tomato sauce. Sprinkle with parsley.

Baked Haddock Cottage Style

2 haddock fillets, 3-1/2 pounds total
1/2 cup butter
salt and pepper to taste
juice of 1 lemon
12 common crackers, crushed
6 scallions, thinly sliced
6 mushrooms, minced
2 tablespoons minced parsley
16 thin slices bacon

Preheat oven to 400°F. Sandwich fillets. Place in buttered baking pan; season with salt, pepper, and lemon juice. Combine crackers, scallions, mushrooms, and parsley. Melt butter, stir in crumb mixture, and spread over fish. Lay bacon slices on top. Bake.

9 Fish Dishes

Baked Fresh
Mackerel
Cape Cod

1/2 pound bacon, julienne
1 bunch scallions, thinly sliced
4 mackerel fillets
  salt and pepper to taste
  juice of 1 lemon
1 pound sliced mushrooms
4 tomatoes, peeled, diced
4 bay leaves
  minced parsley
12 clams in the shell

Preheat oven to 400°F. Saute bacon and scallions in large baking pan until soft but not brown. Lift out and reserve. Arrange fillets in pan and season with salt, pepper, and lemon juice. Spread with scallions, bacon, mushrooms, tomatoes, bay leaves, and parsley. Open clams, leaving meat in one shell, and arrange around the fish. Cover and bake 20 minutes.

Salmon
Timbales

2 pounds fresh salmon
2 cups dry white wine
1 teaspoon minced shallots
1 teaspoon lemon juice
2 egg yolks
1 teaspoon salt
  cayenne pepper to taste
2 teaspoons cornstarch
1-1/3 cups milk
1/2 cup heavy cream, whipped
2 cups cream sauce
  cooked asparagus

Poach salmon in wine, shallots, and water to cover. Remove any skin and bones and grind meat finely in processor with lemon juice and egg yolks. Season with salt and pepper. Add cornstarch and mix well. Add milk and mix. Cool and fold in whipped cream. Fill individual molds. Bake in bain marie. Unmold and serve with cream sauce and asparagus.

Fish and Spinach Casserole with Noodles

6 fish fillets, 1-1/2 pounds each
2 tablespoons minced shallots
    salt and pepper to taste
1/2 cup dry white wine
6 tablespoons butter
3 tablespoons flour
2 cups milk
    Tabasco to taste
    nutmeg to taste
2 egg yolks
1/4 pound fine or medium noodles, cooked
1 pound spinach, cooked, drained, minced
2 tablespoons grated Parmesan

Preheat oven to 400°F. Split fillets down center line and fold in half. Butter a baking dish and place fillets in one layer. Sprinkle with shallots, salt, pepper, and wine. Cover and bake. Transfer fish to a platter and keep warm. Reduce liquid by 1/2. Melt butter in a skillet, add flour, and cook roux. Add milk, salt, pepper,

Tabasco, nutmeg, and fish liquor. Simmer 5 minutes. Remove from heat and thicken with egg yolks. Toss noodles with 1 tablespoon butter. Reheat spinach in 1 tablespoon butter and season with salt and pepper. Spoon noodles into bottom of baking dish. Spoon spinach over noodles and arrange fish on top. Spoon sauce over fish and sprinkle with cheese.

Espadon en Brochettes
Swordfish on Skewers

2 pounds swordfish, 1-1/2-inch cubes
1 cup olive oil
1/4 teaspoon pepper
1 tablespoon minced parsley
    salt to taste
1 cucumber, 1/8-inch thick slices
    anchovy butter

Marinate fish in olive oil, pepper, parsley, and salt. Salt cucumbers and drain 30 minutes. Skewer fish and cucumbers and grill. Serve with anchovy butter.

Oriental Shrimp Omelets

8 slices bacon, diced
1-1/2 cups minced onion
2 cups cooked, diced shrimp
3/4 cup bean sprouts
6 eggs, beaten
1 quart cooking oil
1 cup beef bouillon
1 tablespoon cornstarch
2 teaspoons soy sauce

Saute bacon in skillet until crisp. Add onion and cook until tender. Add shrimp and bean sprouts. Add shrimp mixture to eggs. Heat oil in a skillet and drop mixture in 1/4-cup portions into oil to make small omelets. Brown on both sides. Drain. Combine bouillon, cornstarch, and soy sauce. Simmer until thickened. Serve with omelets.

Shrimp with Sour Cream

4 tablespoons butter
1 cup minced onion
1 cup minced carrot
1 cup minced celery
1 cup minced green pepper
1 cup minced green beans
1 cup minced red pepper
salt and cayenne to taste
2 tablespoons curry powder
1 teaspoon nutmeg
1/2 teaspoon mace
4 tablespoons flour
3 cups sour cream
1 tablespoon paprika
4 cups shelled shrimp
2 cups saffron rice

In a heavy pot, melt butter and add vegetables in layers as listed. Season with salt and cayenne. Cover and cook until soft. Remove from heat and stir in curry powder, nutmeg, mace, and flour. Stir in sour cream and paprika. Heat. Add shrimp and cook. Serve with saffron rice.

Shrimp and Corn Casserole

1-1/2 pounds peeled shrimp
   3 tablespoons butter
  1/2 teaspoon salt
     pepper and cayenne to taste
  1/4 cup minced onion
2-1/2 cups corn, drained
   8 stuffed olives, sliced
   1 cup cream
     minced parsley

Saute shrimp in butter until pink. Season with salt and pepper. Add onion and simmer 1 minute longer. Add corn, olives, and cream. Heat and serve sprinkled with parsley.

Shrimp Bel Paese

2 pounds raw shrimp, peeled, deveined
1 cup clam juice
3 lemon slices
  piece of crushed garlic
6 thin slices onion
2/3 cup sherry
1 cup grated Bel Paese

Combine shrimp, clam juice, water to cover, lemon, garlic, and onion. Bring to a boil and drain. Split shrimp and place in a casserole. Pour on sherry and sprinkle with cheese. Broil until cheese is melted and golden.

9 Fish Dishes

Chicken, Broccoli, and Noodle Casserole

3 cups poached, diced chicken

4 cups supreme sauce

1 bunch broccoli, broken into florets, cooked

salt and pepper to taste

pinch of nutmeg

1/4 pound fine or medium noodles, cooked

1/4 cup grated Gruyere or Parmesan

Combine the chicken, 2 cups of sauce, broccoli, salt, pepper, and nutmeg. Arrange noodles in a buttered baking dish. Top with chicken. Pour remaining sauce over all and sprinkle with cheese. Glaze.

Chapter 10

Meat & Poultry Dishes

Because brunches often serve as lunch for many customers, you will be wise to offer more substantial fare. Poultry and meats can both be used to provide low-cost casseroles with high profit potential. Again, you can use leftovers to stretch your food budget.

Chicken Saute Washington

2 1/2-pound chickens, cut up
    salt and pepper to taste
2 tablespoons butter
1 tablespoon minced shallots
2 tablespoons bourbon
2 cups heavy cream
10 ounces cooked corn

Sprinkle chicken with salt and pepper. Saute in butter until golden and cooked. Remove chicken, pour off fat, and add shallots. Cook until soft. Add whiskey and deglaze pan. Add cream, salt, and pepper. Reduce to coating consistency. Add corn and heat. Pour over chicken and serve.

Creamed Chicken Chestershire

3 cups cooked, diced chicken
1 cup light cream
2 cups Bechamel sauce
4 English muffins
8 thin rounds cheddar
    paprika

Simmer chicken and cream for 10 minutes. Stir in Bechamel. Split muffins, remove soft centers, and toast. Butter lightly. Arrange on a platter. Fill with chicken, place a slice of cheese on each, and dust with paprika. Glaze.

Chicken, Oyster, and Cornbread Shortcake

2 cups Veloute sauce
salt, cayenne, and lemon juice to taste
12 oysters
1-1/2 cups cooked chicken, 3/4-inch cubes
4 4-inch squares warm cornbread
1 tablespoon minced parsley
2 tablespoons minced pimiento

Season Veloute with salt, cayenne, and lemon juice. Poach oysters until plump. Drain and add to sauce. Fold in chicken and correct seasoning. Cut cornbread squares in half horizontally. Spoon some of the chicken mixture over the bottom half. Replace top and spoon on more of the sauce. Sprinkle with parsley and pimiento and serve.

Chicken Livers in Red Wine

1/2 pound button mushroom caps
2 peppers, minced
3 tablespoons butter
1-1/2 pounds chicken livers
4 tablespoons butter
1/2 cup red wine
1 bay leaf
salt and pepper to taste
hot buttered toast

Saute mushrooms and peppers in butter until soft. Saute chicken livers in butter until browned, but still rare. Combine with mushroom mixture, wine, bay leaf, salt, and pepper. Simmer 10 minutes and serve on toast.

Meat & Poultry
10

Brochettes de Foies de Volailles

Chicken Liver Brochettes

1 pound chicken livers, halved
1/4 cup butter
squares of blanched lean bacon
mushroom caps, sauteed in butter
melted butter
bread crumbs

Saute livers in butter until browned, but still rare. Thread on skewers alternating with bacon and mushrooms. Sprinkle with butter and roll in bread crumbs. Broil.

Chicken Livers and Grapes

4 tablespoons butter
1-1/2 pounds chicken livers
1/2 pound seedless green grapes
1/2 cup port
3 cups cooked brown rice
small bunch of grapes

Saute livers in butter until browned, but still rare. Add grapes and port and simmer 4 minutes. Remove grapes and livers to a serving plate. Surround with rice and garnish with grapes.

Armenian Rice with Chicken Livers

12 chicken livers, halved
8 tablespoons butter
2 tablespoons minced onion
2 teaspoons minced garlic
1/4 cup sliced mushrooms
1 green pepper, shredded
2 cups rice
2 tablespoons tomato paste
2 teaspoons glace de viande
4 cups chicken stock
  salt and pepper to taste
  chili pepper to taste
1/2 teaspoon dry mustard
2 tablespoons peach preserves
1 eggplant, 1/2-inch slices, salted
4 tablespoons olive oil
1/2 cup toasted blanched almonds
2 apples, peeled, cored, 1/2-inch slices
2 bermuda onions, 1/2-inch slices
3 tomatoes, peeled, 1/2-inch slices
1 green pepper, finely sliced
1 pimiento, sliced
1/2 pound sliced bacon, grilled

Saute livers in 4 tablespoons butter until brown and remove. Add onion and garlic and cook until soft. Add mushrooms and green pepper and cook 2 minutes. Add rice and cook 3 minutes. Stir in tomato paste, glace de viande, chicken stock, salt, pepper, chili pepper, mustard, and preserves and cook until tender. Drain eggplant and saute in olive oil. Add to rice with almonds. Heat 4 tablespoons of butter and brown apple and onion slices. Add to rice with tomatoes, leaving butter in pan. Saute peppers in same pan and add to rice. Cut chicken livers into thick slices and add to rice with pimientos. Cover and warm over low heat. Garnish with bacon.

Beef Stroganoff

1 pound lean beef filet, 1/4-inch strips
1 tablespoon paprika
3 tablespoons vegetable oil
1/4 pound mushrooms, thinly sliced
1 cup dry sherry
1/2 cup beef stock
1 cup sour cream
1 teaspoon lemon juice
salt to taste
fine noodles, cooked

Dust beef with paprika. Saute in oil until just browned. Remove from pan. Saute mushrooms in pan and remove. Add sherry and reduce to 1/2 cup. Add beef stock and boil for 5 minutes. Reduce to 3/4 cup. Remove from heat and add sour cream, lemon juice, and salt. Return mushrooms and meat to pan and reheat, but do not boil. Serve over noodles.

Hachis de Boeuf Parmentier

Beef and Potato Hash

6 medium baking potatoes, baked
3 tablespoons butter
1 pound roast beef, diced 1/4 inch
4 tablespoons minced onions
2 teaspoons butter
1 tablespoon minced parsley
1/2 teaspoon vinegar
1 cup Lyonnaise sauce

Cut off tops of potatoes and scoop out pulp, reserving shells and tops. Mash potato pulp with butter and stir in beef. Saute onion in butter. Stir into potato with parsley and vinegar. Stir in Lyonnaise sauce. Stuff potato shells, put on caps, and reheat in oven.

Omelette Ropa Vieja
*Cuban "Old Clothes"
Omelet*
(See page 36.)

Princess Omelet
(See page 33.)

Sausages and Apples
(See page 93.)

Oeufs sur le Plat aux
Haricot de Lima
*Shirred Eggs with Lima
Beans*
(See page 22.)

Oeufs Farcis a la
Hollandaise
*Stuffed Eggs
Hollandaise*
(See page 9.)

Hachis de Boeuf
Parmentier
Beef and Potato Hash
(See page 90.)

Muenster and
Caraway Souffle
(See page 56.)

Oeufs sur le Plat
Flamenco
Shirred Eggs Flamenco
(See page 23.)

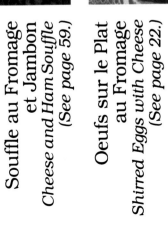

Souffle au Fromage
et Jambon
Cheese and Ham Souffle
(See page 59.)

Oeufs sur le Plat
au Fromage
Shirred Eggs with Cheese
(See page 22.)

Salisbury Steak with
Fried Eggs
(See page 40.)

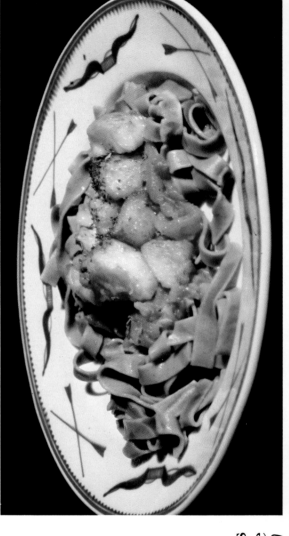

Spinach Noodles
with Scallops Provencale
(See page 79.)

Eggs Massena
(See page 2.)

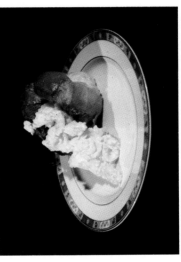

Popovers with
Scrambled Eggs
(See page 41.)

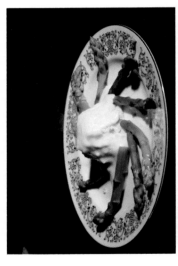

Salmon Timbales
(See page 80.)

Oeufs a la Mozart
Hard Cooked Eggs, Mozart
(See page 15.)

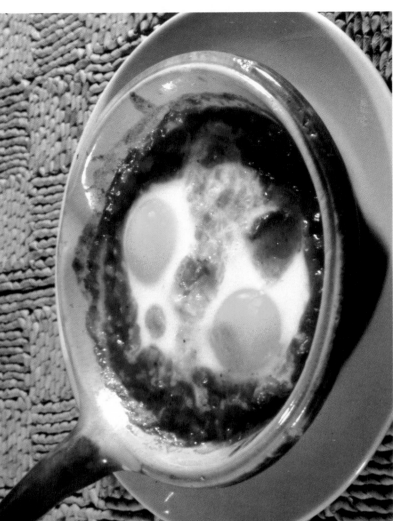

Oeufs sur le Plat
Lyonnaise
Shirred Eggs Lyonnaise
Style
(See page 19.)

in butter until soft. Stir into pan juices from braising and reheat. Cut beef into 1/2-inch slices and serve sauce on the side.

Creamed Mushrooms and Dried Beef

1/2 pound mushrooms, julienne
2 tablespoons butter
2 cups Bechamel sauce
4 ounces dried beef
2 ounces pimientos, drained
2 cups grated cheddar
pinch each of grated nutmeg and cayenne
salt and pepper to taste
buttered toast points

Saute mushrooms in butter until they give up their liquid. Stir in the sauce, beef, and pimientos. Remove from heat and fold in the cheese, nutmeg, and cayenne. Correct seasoning. Serve on toast points.

Olive Beef Roll

2 pounds boneless round steak
1 teaspoon salt
1 teaspoon paprika
1/4 teaspoon pepper
8 ounces thinly sliced mushrooms
1-1/4 cups thinly sliced onions
2/3 cup fine dry bread crumbs
1/2 cup melted butter
1 tablespoon boiling water
1 egg
1 cup large Spanish olives
1/4 cup butter
1 cup dry red wine
2 tablespoons butter

Preheat oven to 325°F. Remove fat from meat and pound meat to 1/4-inch thickness. Rub salt, paprika, and pepper into both sides of the meat. Spread 4 ounces mushrooms, 1 cup onions, and bread crumbs over the meat. Combine butter, water, and egg in a bowl. Whisk until foamy. Pour over meat. Line olives on meat end to end. Roll meat from long side, skewer, and tie. Saute in butter until browned. Remove to a casserole. Add wine to skillet and deglaze. Pour over roll and braise until tender. Saute remaining mushrooms and onions

broil until brown. Saute celery and onion in butter until soft. Add flour and cook 3 minutes. Stir in reserved beef broth and cream. Simmer until thick and smooth. Add sausage and beef. Cook noodles in water flavored with curry powder. Add pea pods and celery to meat mixture. Serve over noodles.

Casserole of Sweetbreads and Dried Beef

2 pairs blanched sweetbreads, thinly sliced

3 tablespoons butter

4 ounces dried beef, julienne

3 cups thin cream sauce

2-1/2 cups artichoke hearts, cooked

2 tablespoons each, grated Parmesan and Gruyere

Saute sweetbreads in butter until golden. Add beef and heat. Stir in sauce and correct seasoning. Place artichoke hearts in casserole and spoon mixture over them. Sprinkle with cheeses and bake until bubbly.

Creamed Beef and Sausage over Curried Noodles

2 tablespoons butter

2 tablespoons vegetable oil

2 pounds beef round, 1-inch cubes

4 cups water

2 bay leaves

1 teaspoon salt

1 pound kielbasa

1 cup water

1 cup sliced celery

3/4 cup chopped onion

1/4 cup butter

6 tablespoons flour

1/2 cup heavy cream

8 ounces egg noodles

1/2 teaspoon curry powder

8 ounces snow pea pods

1/2 cup sliced celery

Heat butter and oil in skillet and brown beef on all sides. Add water, bay leaves, and salt. Braise until tender. Drain, reserving 3 cups broth. Simmer sausage in water for 10 minutes. Cut into 1/2-inch slices and paprika, hot peppers, thyme, rosemary, and tomatoes. Return sausages to pan and cook over medium heat until tomato juices evaporate. Correct seasoning. Sprinkle with pimiento, garlic, and parsley.

Sausages and Apples

1 pound pork sausage links
1 cup maple syrup
1/2 cup white vinegar
4 medium apples, cored, 1/2-inch slices

Fry sausages and drain. Heat syrup and vinegar in a saucepan to boiling. Lower heat. Add apples and cook until tender crisp. Remove apples to a platter and arrange with sausages.

Sausages a la Campagnarde

3 tomatoes, chopped
1/4 cup olive oil
6 Italian sweet sausages
2 tablespoons dry white wine
1 large onion, thinly sliced
1 teaspoon minced garlic
1/2 pound thinly sliced mushrooms
2 green peppers, peeled, sliced
salt and pepper to taste
1/2 teaspoon paprika
1/4 teaspoon hot pepper
1/4 teaspoon dried thyme
1/4 teaspoon dried rosemary
1/2 cup diced pimiento
2 tablespoons minced garlic
2 tablespoons minced parsley

Place tomatoes in a colander over a bowl and sprinkle with salt. Drain for 30 minutes. Heat 2 tablespoons of oil and add sausages and wine. Cover and cook over low heat until browned. Remove to a plate and discard fat. Add remaining oil and saute onion and garlic until soft. Add mushrooms and peppers and season with salt and pepper. Cook 3 to 4 minutes. Add

Saute de Veau
a la Creme
Sauteed Veal with Cream

2 pounds leg of veal, 1-1/2-inch cubes

6 tablespoons butter

1/3 cup cognac

1 onion, minced

1/4 pound mushrooms, thinly sliced

1 teaspoon lemon juice

salt and pepper to taste

1 cup white raisins, soaked in 1/2 cup dry sherry

1 teaspoon minced garlic

2 teaspoons tomato paste

1 teaspoon meat glaze

3 tablespoons flour

1 cup chicken stock

1 cup sour cream

1/2 cup heavy cream, whipped

2 tablespoons minced chives

Preheat oven to 350°F. Brown veal in 3 tablespoons butter. Remove to a casserole. Add cognac to pan and ignite. Deglaze. Add remaining butter and onions to pan and cook 2 minutes. Add mushrooms, lemon juice, salt, and pepper and cook 3 minutes. Add raisins, sherry, and garlic and simmer 5 minutes. Add tomato paste, meat glaze, and flour and mix well. Stir in chicken stock and bring to a boil. Slowly mix in sour cream. Add to veal and bake for 45 minutes. When tender, fold in whipped cream. Sprinkle with chives.

Veal and
Sausage Ragout

3 onions, sliced

2 tablespoons butter

1 pound veal, 3/4-inch cubes

2 tablespoons paprika

2 tomatoes, quartered

1 green pepper, sliced

1/2 pound kielbasa, sliced

1 cup sour cream

Saute onions in butter until soft. Add veal and paprika. Saute 10 minutes. Add tomatoes, pepper, and sausage. Simmer until tender. Remove from heat. Stir in sour cream.

Tendrons de Veau a l'Estragon

Breast of Veal with Tarragon

2 pounds breast of veal, boned
6 tablespoons clarified butter
3 tablespoons flour
1/2 cup white wine
1/2 cup water
1 teaspoon tarragon
salt and pepper to taste
1 teaspoon fresh tarragon

Preheat oven to 300°F. Cut veal into strips 1 by 3 inches. Saute in butter until golden. Sprinkle with flour and cook until lightly browned. Add wine and water and deglaze. Simmer 5 minutes. Transfer to a casserole and bring to a boil. Season with tarragon, salt, and pepper. Bake 1-1/2 hours. Add fresh tarragon 10 minutes before it is finished.

Blanquette de Veau Menagere

Veal Stew

3 pounds breast of veal, 2-inch cubes
12 small white onions
6 tablespoons butter
2 tablespoons flour
water
bouquet garni
salt and pepper to taste
2 egg yolks
juice of 1/2 lemon
1/4 cup heavy cream
rice or steamed potatoes

Saute veal with onions in butter until golden. Sprinkle with flour, stir well, and add water to cover. Add bouquet garni, salt, and pepper. Simmer 1-1/2 hours or until tender. Remove meat and onions to a hot serving bowl. In a bowl, combine egg yolks, lemon juice, and cream. Whisk into the sauce and bring just to a boil. Pass through a sieve over the meat and onions. Serve with rice or potatoes.

Minuten Fleisch

Minute Steak

1-1/2 pounds veal cutlets
  salt and pepper to taste
2/3 cup red wine
  flour
1-1/2 cups brown stock
  juice of 1 lemon
2 sprigs parsley

Pound veal thin. Season with salt and pepper, and marinate in wine for 6 hours. Drain, dust with flour, and arrange in buttered casserole in one layer. Pour on stock and lemon juice, and add parsley. Cover and simmer until tender.

Sweetbread and Oyster Casserole

8 tablespoons butter
2 tablespoons minced onions
2 tablespoons minced celery
2 tablespoons minced carrots
2 pounds sweetbreads, blanched, peeled

3/4 cup pale dry sherry
4 sprigs parsley
1 bay leaf
1 pint oysters
6 tablespoons flour
1/2 cup heavy cream
2 tablespoons dry Madeira
  pinch of mace
1 hard cooked egg, minced

Melt 4 tablespoons butter in a casserole and cook the onions, celery, and carrots until soft. Add sweetbreads and cook 5 minutes. Add sherry, parsley, and bay leaf. Braise 30 minutes. Remove sweetbreads and cut into 1/4-inch thick slices. Strain casserole mixture pressing on vegetables. Measure liquid and add enough oyster liquor to make 2 cups. Melt 4 tablespoons butter in a skillet, and stir in flour and cooking liquid. Cook, stirring until thick and smooth. Simmer 3 minutes. Add heavy cream, Madeira, and mace. Remove from heat and add sweetbreads and oysters. Mix to coat. Put into casserole and bake 10 minutes or until oysters are cooked. Sprinkle with minced egg and serve.

Beurre de Maitre d'Hotel

1/2 pound butter
1 tablespoon minced parsley
salt and pepper to taste
few drops lemon juice

Cream the butter and work in parsley, salt, pepper, and lemon juice. Shape into a log and chill.

Ham Hash

3 tablespoons butter
2 cups finely chopped ham
2 cups chopped cooked potato
1 cup sour cream
salt and pepper to taste
minced chives

In a skillet, melt butter and add ham and potatoes. Add sour cream, salt, and pepper. Heat until hot but not boiling. Garnish with chives.

Brochettes de Foie de Veau

Calves Liver Skewers

2 pounds calves' livers
salt and pepper to taste
2 tablespoons butter
1 pound blanched salt pork, 2-inch cubes
18 mushroom caps, sauteed in butter
1 cup duxelles sauce
1 cup bread crumbs
melted butter
Maitre d'Hotel butter

Cut liver into 2-inch cubes. Season with salt and pepper. Toss in butter in skillet to firm. Combine liver, salt pork, mushroom caps, and duxelles. Toss well. Skewer on bamboo skewers. Sprinkle generously with crumbs and sprinkle with butter. Brown under a broiler. Serve with slices of Maitre d'Hotel butter (see following recipe).

Meat & Poultry
10

Chapter 11

Basic Sauces & Preparations

A lthough any qualified chef will know how to make these sauces, it is not unusual for any of us to need a reminder about the details. In some kitchens these preparations always will be on hand, but in others special preparations may need to be made for the dishes in this book.

The recipes in this chapter will serve as reminders for the chef who is familiar with the sauces, and for those chefs who are not, perhaps, as inspiration for increasing their repertoire. And by including these recipes, the chef will not need to hunt for a particular recipe during what is normally a hectic day.

Bechamel Sauce

2 tablespoons butter
1 tablespoon minced onion
4 tablespoons flour
3 cups milk, scalded
1/4 teaspoon salt
3 white peppercorns
sprig of parsley
pinch of grated nutmeg

Melt the butter in a saucepan. Saute the onion until soft. Add flour and cook roux slowly until it just starts to turn golden. Add milk gradually and cook, stirring, until thick and smooth. Season with salt, peppercorns, parsley, and nutmeg. Stirring often, cook slowly for 30 minutes or until reduced to two-thirds of original quantity. Strain. Yields 2 cups.

Sauce Creme

2 cups Bechamel sauce
1/2 cup heavy cream
salt to taste
lemon juice to taste

Reduce Bechamel to 1-1/2 cups and add heavy cream. Correct seasoning with salt and lemon juice and strain.

Veloute Sauce

2 tablespoons butter
4 tablespoons flour
3 cups hot fish or chicken stock
3 white peppercorns
salt to taste
sprig of parsley
1/2 cup mushroom peelings and stems

In a saucepan, melt butter and add flour. Cook roux, stirring, until it just starts to turn golden. Gradually add stock, stirring vigorously. Add seasonings. Simmer, stirring, until reduced to two-thirds of original quantity. Strain and correct seasonings.

Sauce Allemande

2 egg yolks, lightly beaten
4 tablespoons heavy cream
2 cups Supreme sauce, heated

Combine egg yolks, 2 tablespoons heavy cream, and hot sauce. Heat, stirring, until it just reaches the boil. Stir in remaining cream and strain.

Sauce Mornay

3 egg yolks
1/2 cup heavy cream
2 cups hot Bechamel sauce
2 tablespoons grated Swiss or Parmesan
2 tablespoons butter

Combine egg yolks with cream and add to hot Bechamel. Cook, stirring, until it just reaches the boiling point. Stir in cheese and butter. Strain.

Sauce Supreme

2 cups chicken stock
3 sliced mushrooms
1 cup Veloute sauce
1 cup heavy cream
salt and cayenne to taste

In a saucepan, cook the stock and mushrooms until reduced to one-third of the original quantity. Add Veloute and bring to a boil. Stir in heavy cream. Strain and correct seasoning.

Sauce Espaganole

1/2 cup clarified butter
1 small carrot, minced
2 medium onions, minced
1/2 cup flour
3 cups brown stock
1 clove garlic, crushed
1 stalk celery
3 sprigs parsley
1 small bay leaf
   pinch of thyme
3 cups hot brown stock
1/2 cup tomato puree
2 cups hot brown stock

In a saucepan, melt the butter. Add the carrot and onions and cook until they start to brown. Add flour and cook, stirring, until the roux is a good deep brown. Add 3 cups of stock, garlic, and a faggot made from celery, parsley, bay leaf, and thyme. Cook, stirring often, until the mixture thickens. Add 3 more cups of stock. Cook slowly for 1-1/2 hours or until reduced to 3 cups. As the sauce cooks, skim off any excess fat. Add tomato puree and cook 20 minutes. Strain. Add the remaining hot stock and simmer 1 hour or until reduced to 4 cups. Strain and cool.

Demi-Glace Sauce

1-1/2 cups Espagnole sauce
1-1/2 cups beef stock
5 tablespoons dry sherry

In a saucepan, combine the sauce and stock. Simmer until reduced to 1-1/2 cups. Remove from heat. Stir in sherry and strain.

Tomato Sauce

1 quart tomatoes, plum preferred
1 onion, halved
1 teaspoon salt
1/4 pound butter
1 teaspoon sugar

Cut tomatoes into chunks and place in pan over medium heat. Cover and simmer 10 minutes, stirring occasionally. Put tomatoes through a food mill or processor and then push them through a sieve. Discard seeds and skins. Put into a clean pot with the onion, salt, butter, and sugar. Simmer gently 45 minutes or until thick and smooth. Discard onion and correct seasoning.   101

Duxelles Sauce

1 tablespoon minced shallots
3 tablespoons butter
1 cup minced mushrooms
1/2 cup dry white wine
3/4 cup Demi-glace sauce
1/2 cup tomato puree
   salt and pepper to taste
2 tablespoons butter
1 tablespoon minced parsley

Saute shallots in butter until soft. Stir in mushrooms and cook until tender. Add wine and simmer until almost evaporated. Add sauce and tomato puree and cook 3 minutes. Season with salt and pepper. Swirl in butter and parsley before serving.

Duxelles II

1 tablespoon minced shallots
3 tablespoons butter
1 cup minced mushrooms
1 cup Bechamel sauce
   salt and pepper to taste

Saute shallots in butter until soft. Add mushrooms and cook until the liquid has evaporated. Stir in Bechamel and reheat. Correct seasoning.

Sauce Lyonnaise

1/2 cup minced onions
2 tablespoons butter
4 tablespoons dry white wine
1/2 cup wine vinegar
3 cups Demi-glace sauce
   salt and pepper to taste

Lightly brown onions in the butter. Add wine and vinegar and cook until reduced by one-third. Stir in sauce and simmer 30 minutes. Correct seasoning. Serve strained or unstrained.

Sauce Hollandaise

3 egg yolks
1 tablespoon water
1/2 cup butter
   salt to taste
   lemon juice to taste

In a saucepan, combine egg yolks and water and whisk until light. Put over medium heat and start beating in butter, making sure that it emulsifies before adding more. When completely incorporated, correct seasoning.

Bearnaise Sauce

2 teaspoons tarragon

2 teaspoons chervil

2 shallots, minced

1/4 cup tarragon vinegar

1/4 cup white wine

3 egg yolks

1 tablespoon water

1/2 cup butter

    salt to taste

    pinch of cayenne

In small saucepan, combine 1 teaspoon tarragon, 1 teaspoon chervil, and shallots. Add vinegar and wine and simmer until reduced to a thick paste. Put tarragon mixture into a saucepan, add egg yolks and water, and whisk until fluffy. Add butter to form a sauce as with Hollandaise. When finished, strain. Stir in remaining tarragon and chervil. Correct seasoning.

Dessert Crepes

2/3 cup flour

1 tablespoon sugar

    pinch of salt

2 whole eggs

2 egg yolks

1-3/4 cups milk

2 tablespoons melted butter

1 tablespoon rum or cognac

In a bowl, combine flour, sugar, and salt. Combine eggs and egg yolks with flour. Gradually add milk, stirring until smooth. Add butter and liquor and let batter rest for 2 hours. Strain.

Entree Crepes

3/4 cup sifted flour

3 eggs

1 cup milk

1/2 teaspoon salt

4 tablespoons melted butter

Place flour in a bowl and add eggs, working mixture into a paste. Stir in the milk gradually to avoid lumps. Add salt and butter. Strain and let rest 2 hours.

Index